*To Jimmy —
Your Mom and Dad used this book
last Lent, and wanted you to have a copy.*

THROUGH LENT WITH

JOHN'S PEOPLE

With all best wishes,

MR. THOMAS GARRY, OP

Tom Garry

2017
DNS PUBLICATIONS

Through Lent with John's People
by Mr. Thomas Garry, OP

NIHIL OBSTAT
Rev. Christopher M. Ciccarino, S.S.L, S.T.D.
Censor Librorum
September 16, 2016

IMPRIMATUR
+Most Reverend John J. Myers, J.C.D., D.D.
Archbishop of Newark
October 20, 2016

Printed in the United States of America

DNS PUBLICATIONS

Dominican Nuns of Summit
543 Springfield Avenue
Summit, New Jersey 07901
www.nunsopsummit.org

ISBN: 0692595120
ISBN-13: 978-0692595121

Cover Image: *The Exhortation to the Apostles* by James Tissot. Brooklyn Museum.

Dedication

To Sandy, my steadfast companion
through all of life's seasons

Contents

INTRODUCTION

The Gospel of St. John is an inquiry into – and ultimately a manifesto of – identity.

Throughout its 21 chapters, people ask, speculate, and argue about who Jesus is. Not infrequently, the Lord is the one asking the questions as a way of inviting those He encounters to faith. When He meets the man born blind after He has given him the gift of sight, Jesus asks, "Do you believe in the Son of Man?" (John 9:35) When so many of His early followers leave because they cannot accept His teaching that, "unless you eat the flesh of the Son of Man and drink his blood, you have no life in you," He asks the Twelve, "Do you also wish to go away?" (John 6:67) Peter replies with words that answer not only that question but the larger question of who Jesus is: "Lord, to whom can we go? You have the words of eternal life. We have come to believe and know that you are the Holy One of God." (John 6:68-69) When He comes to Martha as she mourns her brother Lazarus, who was buried four days before, He tells her that He is "the resurrection and the life," and that those who believe in Him will never die. Then Jesus asks her: "Do you believe this?" (John 11:24-26)

And by answering those questions that identify and define Jesus, those whom He questions identify and define themselves.

1

The same task – and the same invitation to faith – awaits each of us this Lent. We, too, must decide who Jesus is to us, and who we are or will strive to be as a result.

This book was written to facilitate that process of inquiry and reflection by providing a brief passage from John's Gospel for each of the 40 days of Lent. The Gospel passage is followed by an essay of approximately 1,000 words that focuses on a person or group of people presented in the Gospel account, which is taken from the New Revised Standard Version – Catholic Edition. The essay considers how that person's or group's experience, situation, or attitude might be similar to our own, or at least instructive for ours. Each day's essay then concludes with a few questions for reflection. This structure offers readers the opportunity to engage this Lent in a version of the ancient Catholic practice of *lectio divina*, and its "four movements" of *lectio* (reading a passage of Scripture), *meditatio* (meditating on that passage), *oratio* (praying about the passage) and *contemplatio* (contemplating on the passage). I am indebted to my sisters and brothers in the Lay Fraternities of St. Dominic for introducing me to this approach, and for emphasizing the importance it held for Dominic himself. Similarly, the book and its structure owe acknowledgment and a debt of gratitude to the Spiritual Exercises of the Jesuits and their founder, St. Ignatius Loyola, in that its encouragement to try to recognize aspects of ourselves in those who encountered the Lord might be considered "quasi-Ignatian."

It is important to address two other issues of identity in this introduction.

The first concerns who the author is, and is not. To start with the latter, I am not a biblical scholar, theologian, member of the clergy, or in any other way someone with formal training or expertise in Scripture or the teaching of the Church. Rather,

I am nothing more (but nothing less) than a layman who strives to be a faithful Catholic and a good husband, father, son, brother, uncle and friend, and who all too often is painfully aware of coming up short in that effort. I hope and believe that everything I have written in this book reflects orthodox Roman Catholic belief and teaching. I also hope that any deficiencies noted will, in charity, be attributed to lack of expertise rather than to any lack of faith or fidelity to the magisterium.

The second pertains to the Gospel's references, often negative, to "the Jews." John's Gospel traditionally has been considered the last of the four Gospels to be written, and biblical scholars tell us that it was composed at a time when there were bitter divisions within the Jewish community between adherents of the synagogue (the majority, who rejected the assertion that Jesus was the Messiah) and the church (the minority, who had come to accept Jesus as Messiah, Lord and Savior). In its 2001 study, "The Jewish People and Their Sacred Scriptures in the Christian Bible," the Pontifical Biblical Commission acknowledged that in John's Gospel, those who oppose Jesus "are often called 'the Jews' without further precision, with the result that an unfavourable judgment is associated with that name." The Commission adds, however, that "there is no question here of anti-Jewish sentiment" and that "this manner of speaking only reflects the clear separation that existed between the Christian and Jewish communities" at the time the Gospel was written. The Commission — whose president was Joseph Cardinal Ratzinger, later Pope Benedict XVI — opens its discussion of John's Gospel by noting, "About the Jews, the Fourth Gospel has a very positive statement, made by Jesus

3

himself in the dialogue with the Samaritan woman: 'Salvation comes from the Jews' (Jn 4:22)."*

This historical context and larger perspective are crucial for contemporary readers who come to John's Gospel aware of the horrific anti-Semitism that has been a stain on Western culture in the intervening centuries, and who rightly are outraged by the extent to which some have sought to justify this terrible prejudice and sin by the spurious accusation that the Jewish people somehow are "Christ killers." The Church has rejected this deicide libel, including – recently – in Pope Benedict XVI's 2011 book, "Jesus of Nazareth." As addressed in this volume's entry for Thursday of the Fifth Week of Lent, Catholic teaching is very clear on the identity of those responsible for the Lord's crucifixion: We all are responsible, due to our sins.

It is my prayer that this book will help readers enter more deeply this Lent not only into a consciousness of that sin, which necessitated the atonement made on the Cross, but also of the innate worth, intrinsic dignity, and great hope we all possess as daughters and sons of a loving and forgiving God.

May our confidence in, and gratitude for, the salvific power of the Passion, Death, and Resurrection of Jesus enable us, like Martha, to respond to Him by saying, "Yes, Lord, I believe that you are the Messiah, the Son of God." (John 11:27).

---

*http://www.vatican.va/roman_curia/congregations/cfaith/pcb_doc uments/rc_con_cfaith_doc_20020212_popolo-ebraico_en.html

ASH WEDNESDAY
JOHN THE BAPTIST

"There was a man sent from God,
whose name was John."
John 1:6

It is easy to believe that John the Baptist was "sent from God." The Gospels tell us this was the case, that he led a prophet's life and died a martyr's death. He is recognized as a saint, with the Church designating feast days to mark both his birth (June 24) and his beheading (August 29).

Even without this scriptural and ecclesiastical assurance, however, John fits our image of someone "sent from God." He rejected the comforts and conventions of his time and place. He withdrew from society, preferring the harsh isolation of the desert. He fashioned his clothes from camel's hair, and subsisted on a diet of locusts and wild honey. And his message was as alarming as his appearance must have been. He called the religious authorities of his day a "brood of vipers," (Matthew 3:7) and spoke of a fast-approaching judgment when the unworthy would be consigned to "burn with unquenchable fire." (Matthew 3:12) He was, in contemporary parlance, a wild man.

How much more difficult it is to accept that there is a man or woman of your name who also was "sent from God." Not just created by God; that is easy for a Christian to fathom and believe. And not just placed here for a certain amount of time to exist in passive fashion, living as good a life as you can

5

manage in your circumstances; that is a minimalistic view of the call and destiny of the faithful. No; the operative word is *sent*. It is a verb laden with implications for our lives.

When we send someone a card or package, we have a specific purpose in mind—to provide encouragement to a loved one struggling with loss, to give a soldier stationed overseas some of the amenities of home, or to get a much-desired toy to a niece or nephew in time to be opened on Christmas morning. That specific purpose is matched by a specific destination. We don't drop an unaddressed letter in the mailbox, or expect UPS or FedEx to deliver a package if we don't fill out the label. Why, then, would we think that in putting us here, God would do so without having a specific reason in mind?

The problem, of course, is that we usually do not know that destination, or would rather not acknowledge and respond to the intimations of grace pointing us toward a destination that doesn't appeal to us.

That's why we have Lent. We are called to a barrenness in which we purposely withdraw from the pleasures that anesthetize us, the satiety that induces torpor, the distractions that justify deferral and evasion. Mark's Gospel tells us that after Jesus was baptized, "And the Spirit immediately drove him out into the wilderness. He was in the wilderness for forty days, tempted by Satan; and he was with the wild beasts; and the angels waited on him." (Mark 1:12-13)

Those baptized in Christ have a duty to follow the newly baptized Christ into our own deserts. We will be tempted, perhaps most strongly by the desire to abandon the austerity of Lent for the ephemeral comforts of "ordinary life." We will be among wild beasts. These will be the unwholesome hungers within us that can become ferocious creatures when not regularly fed and accommodated. But we also will be ministered to by angels, few of whom will be dispatched from celestial realms. Far more will be people already in our lives, whose angelic features were obscured before the asceticism of Lent bestowed its gift of a new acuity of vision.

If John the Baptist is too intimidating a model to contemplate as you embark on your Lenten sojourn, think instead of the drastically more-approachable figures of Jake and Elwood Blues. The John Belushi and Dan Ackroyd characters from the 1980 movie *The Blues Brothers* are as unlikely agents of the Almighty as one can imagine. An ex-con and his sketchy brother scrambling to stay one step ahead of the law, a heavily armed ex-girlfriend, Illinois Nazis, and other dangerous and aggrieved pursuers. And yet, when asked at various points throughout the movie what they are doing, the Brothers reply without the least hesitation, elaboration, or doubt, "We're on a mission from God."

That line invariably draws laughs, even from people who have seen the movie two, three, or more times. We laugh at the nonchalant certitude with which these improbable missioners declare their purpose. But perhaps we also laugh because we're uncomfortable with the notion that one can believe so deeply and know so clearly that they have been put here for a specific reason. We, too, are improbable missioners (at least in our own minds), and this Lent we would be well served to seek the certitude of Jake and Elwood Blue that, "We're on a mission from God."

In the Rite of Baptism, each of us was anointed priest, prophet, and king. The Christian insistence on the intrinsic dignity of every human being—irrespective of any consideration of physical or mental capacity, wealth, race, or social status—is

7

rooted in the knowledge that each of us was created by God and in the faith that each was created to play a unique role in God's plan.

So we, too, are "sent from God." For most, our destination won't be a foreign land and our prophetic office won't involve declaiming in the town square. But when a young mother with a packed schedule finds time to run to the pharmacy to pick up a prescription for an elderly, homebound neighbor, or when a busy executive takes a day off to visit a terminally ill former colleague, is it really too far-fetched to say that they were "sent from God"?

Let us begin our Lenten journey confident that we have been "sent by God," and let us pray that at the end of these 40 days, God will give us the grace to discern through prayer and stillness where He is directing us next.

For Reflection:

1. At what times in my life might I have been "sent from God" to be somewhere, with someone, or to do something? How did I respond to those calls, and what were the results?

2. In what circumstances and settings am I best able to still myself and discern what God may be saying to me? How can I arrange my life this Lent so that I spend more time in those settings and circumstances?

3. Looking deeply within myself, do I have a sense that God is calling me to be somewhere right now?

4. What small service can I do for someone this day or this week that may entail my being "sent from God"?

THURSDAY AFTER ASH WEDNESDAY
JOHN THE BAPTIST

"He came as a witness to testify to the light, so that all might believe through him. He himself was not the light, but he came to testify to the light."
John: 1:7-8

The only people who do more to thwart the evangelical mission of the Church than bad Christians are good Christians.

By the laxness of their practice or their scandalous behavior, the former signal that, for them, there is nothing transformative about the Christian life. But by the self-righteousness and triumphalism with which the latter display their rectitude, they send the message that Christianity, just like every other component of society, has a pecking order, an in-crowd and an out-crowd, and an elite whose distinguishing mark is smug disdain for the less worthy.

These are the people who forget what John the Baptist remembered. They forget that they are not the light, but rather are here to testify to the light. You've seen them on TV and encountered them in your parish. Perhaps, like me, there have been occasions where you've caught a glimpse of them in yourselves. There's the glib televangelist who glories not so much in the Word of God as in the emotional sway that his own words enable him to exercise over his flock. There's "Our Lady of Perpetual Motion," the woman in each parish who chairs pretty much every committee, and wouldn't have it any other way, but whose full schedule always includes time for a recitation of her many contributions and a litany of complaints about all the others who do so little. There's the "rock-solid Catholic," whose conviction extends to the firm belief that those who aren't in absolute agreement with him on every point, not infrequently including the pastor, are of questionable moral character and suspect orthodoxy. And, as noted above, there are times when we ourselves are more focused on sanctimony than sanctity, drawing undue comfort from the fact that we're at Sunday Mass more often than our neighbors, or in one way or another can count ourselves "better Catholics" than someone else.

As we enter Lent, it's worth remembering that Jesus reserved his sharpest rebukes for the self-satisfied and the self-righteous, particularly when they gleefully contrasted their supposed devoutness with the evident faults and failings of others. This is why the Gospel reading for the Ash Wednesday Mass often is from the sixth chapter of Matthew, where Jesus tells His followers:

> Beware of practicing your piety before others in order to be seen by them; for then you have no reward from your Father in heaven. So whenever you give alms, do not sound a trumpet before you, as the hypocrites do in the synagogues and in the streets, so that they may be praised by others. Truly I tell you, they have received their reward. But when you give alms, do not let your left hand know what your right hand is doing, so that your alms may be done in secret; and your Father who sees in secret will reward you.

And whenever you pray, do not be like the hypocrites; for they love to stand and pray in the synagogues and at the street corners, so that they may be seen by others. Truly I tell you, they have received their reward. But whenever you pray, go into your room and shut the door and pray to your Father who is in secret; and your Father who sees in secret will reward you. (Matthew 6:1-6)

Jesus abhorred spiritual exhibitionism so much that after following the above passage by teaching His disciples the Lord's Prayer, he immediately returned to the subject with an injunction particularly relevant to this season:

And whenever you fast, do not look dismal, like the hypocrites, for they disfigure their faces so as to show others that they are fasting. Truly I tell you, they have received their reward. But when you fast, put oil on your head and wash your face, so that your fasting may be seen not by others but by your Father who is in secret; and your Father who sees in secret will reward you. (Matthew 6:16-18)

Most of us work to avoid blatantly "blowing our own horns" about our faith and the ways we put it into practice. But, if we're honest with ourselves, how often do we somehow "let slip" in conversation some good thing that we've done? How often do observant Catholics who are at lunch or dinner with friends on a Friday during Lent order the pasta ("But please make sure there's not any meat sauce on it") with just enough emphasis to let our fellow diners know that our choice wasn't motivated by a hankering for Italian? In the grand scheme of things, these are petty failings, but consider Jesus' warning that they rob our good deeds of whatever merit they otherwise would have warranted in the eyes of God.

St. Ignatius of Loyola founded the Society of Jesus, the Jesuits, in 1539, at a time when the Roman Catholic Church was embattled. The Protestant Reformation already had won, and was continuing to win, millions of adherents throughout Europe. The growth of Protestantism was driven in no small part by people's disgust with the corruption and venality of so many "princes of the Church" who had forgotten that they themselves were not the light but rather were called, like John, to testify to the light.

Ignatius founded the Jesuits to counter the Reformation. And he knew that if that effort were to be successful, his priests and brothers would have to be selfless men, the antithesis of those Church leaders who were concerned chiefly with their own status. So he imparted to his followers the principle that all they do should be done *"ad majorem Dei gloriam"*—"For the greater glory of God."

The Jesuits long since have adopted *"Ad majorem Dei gloriam"* as their motto, and it seems a fitting one for us to adopt this Lent, as well. If we can keep our eyes focused on God's glory, rather than our own, those who cast their gaze our way will be more likely to discern a light shining through (not from) us, and recognize it as that of Jesus, the Light of the World.

For Reflection:

1. Can I recall an instance when I've been guilty of spiritual exhibitionism? What prompted my need to "show off" in that way? Did it yield the results I expected or wanted?

2. What modest act of devotion or service can I perform today or this week in a way that will ensure that no one—other than God—will know that I've done it?

3. How can I strengthen myself through prayer to go through this Lent in an upbeat, cheerful fashion, not complaining about, nor broadcasting, the Lenten sacrifices I am making?

FRIDAY AFTER ASH WEDNESDAY
PRIESTS AND LEVITES

"This is the testimony given by John when the Jews sent priests and Levites from Jerusalem to ask him, 'Who are you?' He confessed and did not deny it, but confessed, 'I am not the Messiah.' And they asked him, 'What then? Are you Elijah?' He said, 'I am not.' 'Are you the prophet?' He answered, 'No.' Then they said to him, 'Who are you? Let us have an answer for those who sent us. What do you say about yourself?' He said, 'I am the voice of one crying out in the wilderness, 'Make straight the way of the Lord,' 'as the prophet Isaiah said.'"

John 1:19-23

They were on Official Business.

Can't you imagine the gusts of self-importance that propelled the priests and Levites through the streets of Jerusalem en route to their interview with John? Surely they moved through the crowds with the peremptory clamor of a rock star's entourage arriving at the concert hall or the security escort accorded a head of state traveling to a summit meeting.

They were, after all, the duly authorized representatives of their society, their religion, *their superiors*, charged with interrogating this man who had the temerity to challenge all they held sacred. It was a high honor and great responsibility. And so they sallied forth from the teeming epicenter of their world to the emptiness of the Judean desert, to confront a wild man in a wild place.

You can't help but wonder if, as these distinguished emissaries moved further from the city gates and deeper into the wasteland, their stride lost some of its earlier assurance, if their righteous indignation wasn't tempered by a growing sense of unease. People in positions of authority are accustomed to dealing with others on their own turf and own terms. This time, however, the priests and Levites had been dispatched far from the Temple precincts where they held sway, far—to use a modern term—from their comfort zone.

No doubt the man they were journeying to meet would prove to be a shameless self-promoter, or, if not a charlatan, a madman whose insanity had manifested itself in spiritual fanaticism. His outrageous criticisms of the religious establishment were all the more scandalous because his father had been one of their own, a priest of Abijah, while his mother was descended from Aaron (Luke 1:5).

So when they reached John, even though they well knew his lineage, they asked the question-cum-accusation that those in power have posed to outsiders in every culture and every age: "Who are you?" You don't need to be a scholar of ancient Greek, capable of translating the Gospel from the original, to appreciate that this question could just as accurately have been rendered, "Who do you think you are?" or, better yet, "*Just* who do you think you are?"

Who are you to set up shop out here in the middle of nowhere and issue a call for repentance, accusing not only ordinary people but also the leaders of our religion of hypocrisy and other sins? If people need to get right with God, they can bring their sacrifices to the Temple. That's the way it works: through us. Who do you think you are? Elijah the Prophet? Maybe even the Messiah himself?

Perhaps some of the priests and Levites asked these questions out of a genuine desire, or fear, that John might indeed be the prophet returned or the promised deliverer of Israel. But more, I suspect, served up their queries with a heavy dose of sarcasm, eager to be the ones to lay low this insolent poseur.

John's flat rejection of any such delusions or aspirations must have left the priestly posse at a loss. They couldn't write him off as a lunatic, and his denials gave them no basis to attack him for fakery or blasphemy. Rather, he wouldn't budge off his message about being the one crying out in the desert, which was true enough, and the need to make straight the way of the Lord.

How wonderful it is to be given a measure of power, and how frustrating it is when others don't realize that their job is to bow to your power, to conform to your sense of how things should be, to answer your questions—and to answer those questions the way you want them answered.

There's something of the priest and Levite in all of us.

When those in authority entrust us with an assignment, it validates our importance. *I* may have nagging doubts about myself, but the people in charge know what they're doing, so if they believe in me, I must be all right. Similarly, power is a great differentiator, elevating us over others and again providing assurance to tamp down the vague insecurities about our worth. And if you want to feel that you truly belong, as we all do, there's no surer way than to act as the guardian and vindicator of the status quo, facing down those who reject that which we so desperately seek to embrace and, even more importantly, be embraced by.

That's one reason we feel uncomfortable around people who are different than us, particularly those who could be like us if they wished but who purposely chose another path. What's wrong with them? Why don't they want all the things that I want, and accept all the beliefs that I accept? Could it be that there's actually something wrong with me, not them? What do they know that I don't?

It's a line of internal questioning that can lead one from a sense of superiority through creeping doubt to outright hatred of those whose alternative approach is seen as a rebuke of one's own blind faith in, and arduous pursuit of, convention.

Of course, what John knew and the priests and Levites didn't, was that he *was* the herald of the Lord, while they were merely the agents of the religious rulers of the day, rulers who in later years would arrange both his beheading and Jesus' crucifixion in a bid to preserve their own power.

The next time we have an opportunity to exercise power, in whatever setting and scale, we would be wise to ask ourselves what need it fulfills in us and whose purpose we're ultimately serving. If not God's, then we're no different than the puffed-up functionaries whose efforts to reveal John's assumed faults merely unmasked their own. Most people who choose different paths than ours won't be prophets, but if we carefully consider the emotions they stir in us, they nonetheless can help us discern valuable truths about what we value, and why.

For Reflection:

1. What makes me feel important, and why? To what degree is my sense of value dependent on others, and does that reflect a healthy attention to the views of the people who matter most to me or an unhealthy need to please others? How can I more fully accept and live the truth that my intrinsic value—and that of others—derives from being a child of God?

2. Whose emissary am I?

3. When I exercise power over others, how often is it to accomplish a worthwhile purpose, to serve a less-worthy purpose, or to serve my ego? What can I learn about myself from the way in which I exercise power and the way it makes me feel?

4. How often do I use a question to make a statement? When I ask a question of someone with whom I disagree, how can I do a better job of truly listening to and considering what they have to say?

5. How do I react to people who have chosen lifestyles and beliefs other than mine? How do those people make me feel, and what can I learn about myself from those feelings?

SATURDAY AFTER ASH WEDNESDAY
ANDREW

"The next day John again was standing with two of his disciples, and as he watched Jesus walk by, he exclaimed, 'Look, here is the Lamb of God!' The two disciples heard him say this, and they followed Jesus. When Jesus turned and saw them following, he said to them, 'What are you looking for?' They said to him, 'Rabbi' (which translated means Teacher), 'where are you staying?' He said to them, 'Come and see.' They came and saw where he was staying, and they remained with him that day. It was about four o'clock in the afternoon. One of the two who heard John speak and followed him was Andrew, Simon Peter's brother. He first found his brother Simon and said to him, 'We have found the Messiah' (which is translated Anointed). He brought Simon to Jesus, who looked at him and said, 'You are Simon son of John. You are to be called Cephas' (which is translated Peter)."
John 1:35-42

"What are you looking for?"

This Lent Jesus asks us the same question He asked Andrew and the Baptist's other, unnamed disciple.

It's a hard question to answer. Inside, we know what we want, but it can be difficult to put it into words. It can be scary to acknowledge how *much* we want given how unlikely it may seem that our hopes will be rewarded. And so we are tempted to play it safe, to temper our expectations. Perhaps we turn things inside out, and give up searching in favor of trying to convince ourselves that what we've found is, indeed, what we had sought. Deep down, we know better, even if we let days become weeks and weeks become months and months become

23

years as we labor to content ourselves with the notion that "close enough is good enough."

But love doesn't—or at least shouldn't—settle for close enough.

From both Hollywood romantic comedies and our own experience, we know the story of the couple that dates for years and years, to the point that family and friends ask, "Are they ever going to tie the knot?" Then, out of nowhere, one of them has a chance encounter with someone they've never met before, or knew only casually back in college or at a prior job, and suddenly the long-standing relationship is over. The man or woman who had that unexpected encounter is engaged to the new love interest, and before you know it, you're going to a wedding.

When our deepest self recognizes the one we're meant to be with, we'll put aside anyone or anything else to be with that person. When this happens in a romantic setting, the joy of the person who has found his or her soul mate is offset by the sorrow of the one left behind. When we find Jesus, however, the people who accompanied us to the point of that encounter share our joy, realizing—as the Baptist did—that their role is to bring us to the Lord. That's why this account of Andrew's becoming a follower of Jesus is so rich in insights into the nature of true discipleship.

Consider, as we have before and will again, the integrity and humility of John. He was doing God's will, fulfilling the demanding, dangerous (and ultimately fatal) role the Almighty had assigned him. He had won attention and a following, and people were beginning to speculate about whether he might be the Messiah. And yet the moment Jesus walked past, he unhesitatingly told those nearest him, "Look, here is the Lamb of God." (John 1:36) He didn't try to hold on to them, or divert their attention from Jesus to keep the focus on himself. Instead, he effectively said, "There's the one you have been seeking. What are you waiting for? Don't stay here with me; go after him."

Andrew and his companion reacted with the alacrity of the lover who has found her soul mate. As the Evangelist writes, "The two disciples heard him say this, and they followed Jesus." How many John the Baptists do we have in our lives? Parents and priests and spouses and friends and co-workers who have pointed us toward Jesus and bid us be quick and unstinting in our pursuit of Him? How many times, hopefully, have we fulfilled that role for others? For all of the "noise" that competes for our attention in modern society, there are plenty of voices that can be heard amid and above the din, saying clearly, "Look, here is the Lamb of God." The first step on the path of discipleship is—emulating Andrew's example—to hear and follow those voices.

Notice what happens next. The Evangelist tells us that as soon as Andrew and his companion started in the Lord's direction, "Jesus turned and saw them following." (John 1:38) If we will take the first step, be it an assured stride or a faltering advance, God will see us and turn toward us. At this point, however, He asks us, as He did Andrew, "What are you looking for?" (John 1:38)

Andrew, like so many of us, had difficulty expressing all that he sought from God, so he answered the Lord's question with a query of his own. "Rabbi," he said, "where are you staying?" (John 1:38) Think of all that Andrew revealed with those few words. First, by addressing Jesus as "Rabbi," or teacher, he acknowledged the nature of the relationship he wanted. He recognized that the Lord was the teacher, the one

25

who would give instruction, while he would be the student, the one who would follow that instruction. Second, his desire to accompany and remain with Jesus was evident is his asking where the Lord was staying. Where will you be, so that I can be sure to be there with you? Even if we can't fully articulate what we hope for and ask of God, our discipleship grows from recognizing that our role is to receive and follow His teachings and, as a result, to stay as close to Him as possible.

Jesus recognized the devotion implicit in Andrew's question and so extended an invitation that He also extends to us: "Come and see." (John 1:39) The Evangelist tells us that Andrew and the other disciple accepted that invitation and spent the day with Jesus. Obviously, what he saw was enough for Andrew. He sought out his brother Simon Peter, told Simon that he had found the Messiah, and "brought Simon to Jesus." (John 1:42) In the true spirit of discipleship, Andrew realized that while intimacy with the Lord is a treasure, it is one that we are meant to share, not hoard. So he began his apostleship by bringing to the Lord the man to whom Christ would entrust the keys to His kingdom.

As we move deeper into Lent, may we draw upon the example of Andrew to follow Christ, learn from Him, dwell with Him, and bring others to Him.

For Reflection:

1. What am I looking for this Lent? How can I better articulate it for myself, express it to God in my prayer, and pursue it through my actions and sacrifices in this holy season?

2. Who is serving as John the Baptist for me this Lent, pointing me toward the Lamb of God? How can I better tune out the noise around me to hear and respond to the voice of that herald?

3. What do I need to leave behind this Lent in order to follow the Lord closely and stay with Him?

4. How can I bring my family members and friends to Jesus by virtue of my witness and my example?

MONDAY, FIRST WEEK OF LENT
PHILIP AND NATHANAEL

"Philip found Nathanael and said to him, 'We have found him about whom Moses in the law and also the prophets wrote, Jesus son of Joseph from Nazareth.' Nathanael said to him, 'Can anything good come out of Nazareth?' Philip said to him, 'Come and see.' When Jesus saw Nathanael coming toward him, he said of him, 'Here is truly an Israelite in whom there is no deceit!' Nathanael asked him, 'Where did you get to know me?' Jesus answered, 'I saw you under the fig tree before Philip called you.' Nathanael replied, 'Rabbi, you are the Son of God! You are the King of Israel!' Jesus answered, 'Do you believe because I told you that I saw you under the fig tree? You will see greater things than these.'"
John 1:45-50

If only we could move as quickly and definitively from cynicism to belief as Nathanael.

His first reaction to Philip's news is familiar enough to us. We've been taught that if something seems too good to be true, it is, and the veracity of that maxim is borne out time and again in our daily lives. Every "revolutionary" diet, "reform" politician, and "unprecedented" investment opportunity that promises to change our lives irrevocably for the better comes up short soon enough, leaving us embarrassed by our initial gullibility and determined not to play the fool again.

How much safer and easier it is to protect ourselves by dismissing implausible people and ideas that come from the margins and to play the high-percentage odds, to stick with the status quo—even if it isn't serving us particularly well.

So we can hardly fault Nathanael for refusing to accept Philip's news that he had met the one promised by Moses and the prophets, and that—to top it off—this Messiah was coming not from on high accompanied by a heavenly host, or even from Jerusalem, but from a backwater hamlet.

What happens next shows that even though Philip had been following Jesus for only a short period at this point, perhaps just several hours, he already had learned the most effective way to bring others to the Lord. When Nathanael hit him with his blow-off question, "Can anything good come out of Nazareth?," Philip didn't respond with indignation. He didn't chide Nathanael, or get into a long argument with him, or cite Scripture passages to prove his point, or tell Nathanael that he was going to burn in Hell for rejecting the true God. Such confrontations between believers and non-believers usually mean the end of a conversation, not the start of a conversion.

Instead of falling into that trap, Philip said simply, "Come and see." He realized that his persuasiveness, his intellect, his fervor wouldn't cause Nathanael to believe, but that encountering Jesus would. In short, he knew that it wasn't his job to *make* people believe in Jesus; his job merely was to show people the way to Jesus. That's a lesson that many committed Christians forget, or perhaps are blinded to by ego. Inviting others to "come and see" means that we humble ourselves by recognizing that we're nothing more (and nothing less) than conduits to the Lord, that we honor others by trusting that something deep within them will recognize and respond to God, and that we pay due reverence to Jesus by acknowledging that He is the one who saves people, not us.

By responding to Nathanael with an invitation rather than an insult, Philip facilitated his friend's encounter with Jesus.

And when that encounter occurred, Jesus said of Nathanael what we hope He will be able to say of us when it is our time to stand before the Lord: That we are people "in whom there is no deceit!' With those words of Jesus, cynicism melted to skepticism, and Nathanael asked, likely with some apprehension, '"Where did you get to know me?"

The Lord's specific response to Nathanael reflects a larger truth for all of us: long before we hear the call to conversion, God has seen us, and has known us, and has marked us as His own. Despite the profundity of that truth, and of the conversion that is about to occur, there is nonetheless something offbeat and funny in the exchange that follows. Jesus explains that before Philip called out to Nathanael, He had seen him under the fig tree. That's all it takes for the dam of uncertainty and resistance to burst. Something overwhelming must have been building within Nathanael, because Jesus' mundane explanation provokes Nathanael's profession, "Rabbi, you are the Son of God! You are the King of Israel!" The Lord's bemusement is evident as he asks Nathanael, "Do you believe because I told you that I saw you under the fig tree? You will see greater things than these."

And Nathanael did, of course. He became a disciple and companion of the Lord at that moment, and subsequently saw Jesus perform miracles, teach the people, institute the Eucharist, undergo arrest and torture, die on the cross, and return to His disciples and then His Father after the resurrection.

There's no question that we, like Nathanael, will see greater things by virtue of our belief in Jesus. There is a question, however, of what it will take for us to believe and trust in Jesus as utterly as Nathanael did. Will our hearts be so full that the merest word of the Lord will be all it takes for us to express

31

without hesitation that Jesus Christ is the Son of God, and to hold fast to that faith come what may?

Or will we be more like Thomas? Even though we have traveled with the Lord, and partaken of His Eucharist, and heard His promises to us, will our personal Calvaries rattle our faith and cause us to reject the assertions of our fellow disciples and demand that God do more, show us more, give us yet another sign? Perhaps. And if that is the case, we can be confident that the Lord will invite us, as He did Thomas, to probe His wounds if that's what it takes to heal ours.

For now, though, let us work to emulate both Philip and Nathanael. When we meet people who greet the call to conversion with cynicism, let us remember that our job is not to win, or convince, or condemn, or cajole. Rather, our job is to invite them to see Jesus, and that's a job usually better accomplished by deeds than words. And when we encounter cynicism and doubt and fear in ourselves, let us open ourselves to the word of God and let it operate within us, so that like Nathanael, we may respond to that word with the utter conviction that, "Rabbi, you are the Son of God."

For Reflection:

1. What emotions emerge when I encounter people who are cynical about or dismissive of the Catholic faith, Christianity in general, or God? What do those emotions tell me about myself, and is there anything about myself I want to change based on those insights?

2. When have I been effective in helping people encounter Jesus, and when have I acted in ways that were counter-productive or ineffective? What do I want to do or say the next time I meet someone who needs to experience the presence of God in his or her life?

3. A simple statement from Jesus prompted Nathanael to profess, "Rabbi, you are the Son of God." What simple words, events, and things in my life prompt me to have such assurance? How can I draw upon the word of God, as Nathanael did, to maintain a faith in Christ as strong as was Nathanael's?

TUESDAY, FIRST WEEK OF LENT
THE WAITERS AT CANA

"On the third day there was a wedding in Cana of Galilee, and the mother of Jesus was there. Jesus and his disciples had also been invited to the wedding. When the wine gave out, the mother of Jesus said to him, 'They have no wine.' And Jesus said to her, 'Woman, what concern is that to you and to me? My hour has not yet come.' His mother said to the servants, 'Do whatever he tells you.' Now standing there were six stone water jars for the Jewish rites of purification, each holding twenty or thirty gallons. Jesus said to them, 'Fill the jars with water.' And they filled them up to the brim. He said to them, 'Now draw some out, and take it to the chief steward.' So they took it. When the steward tasted the water that had become wine, and did not know where it came from (though the servants who had drawn the water knew), the steward called the bridegroom and said to him, 'Everyone serves the good wine first, and then the inferior wine after the guests have become drunk. But you have kept the good wine until now.'"
John 2:1-10

To be a waiter or waitress is to be very aware of a dividing line in life, and of which side of that line you're on. Waiters and waitresses come to a restaurant to work, and to please others. The people they serve come to relax, and to enjoy themselves. The customers have money, and are there to spend it. The waiters need money, and are there to earn it.

Waiting on table means being in constant motion without seeming to rush, being readily available when wanted but unobtrusive otherwise, carrying heavy loads in a way that makes them appear light, being pleasant and responsive to the well-mannered and the foul-tempered alike. It requires transitioning

35

seamlessly dozens of times a night from the heat, din, and frenetic pace of the kitchen to the carefully orchestrated ambiance of the dining rooms. How well a waiter manages those balancing acts determines the size of his tips and the security of his job.

The demands are even greater at weddings. Reception halls promote themselves by promising "an unforgettable experience," "a picture-perfect day," and "flawless events." While much has changed over 2,000 years, we can be confident that the families hosting weddings in Jesus' day had the same level of expectation.

Consider, then, the predicament of the headwaiter and servers at the wedding at Cana. They were running out of wine, which meant a humiliated host and angry guests. Their reputations would be ruined, and no doubt there would be a squabble with the family over the final bill. In the midst of scrambling to find a solution, one of the guests inserts herself into the situation. But all she has to offer is the direction to listen to her son, who clearly does not want to be drawn into the mess. And when He finally yields to His mother's importuning, He focuses not on the wine, but on the ceremonial water jars! What a senseless distraction . . . until, of course, the headwaiter tastes what's been drawn from those newly filled jars.

We all spend at least part of our lives as waiters, working hard to meet the needs of others, and engaging in balancing acts to accomplish all we need to do. Sometimes with justification and more often with a sense of self-pity, we can feel resentment toward those we serve. Sometimes they can seem so oblivious to all that we're doing. The teenaged children who don't appreciate how hard their parents work to provide a good home for them; the parents who scowl at a B+ on a report card without knowing how much study went into earning that grade; the spouse who begrudges long hours in the office rather than realizing that those marathon days pay for what seems like an unending succession of bills; the elderly parent whose dementia means providing constant care but precludes even the occasional expression of gratitude. There are times when it can feel as though we're exhausting ourselves so that others can do as they please, and that—like the servers at Cana—our best efforts just aren't going to be enough.

Since we share the lot of those servers, let's consider what we can learn from their experience.

To start, without these ordinary people doing an ordinary job, no one would have benefited from Jesus' first reported miracle. Note the division of labor. God did His job, changing water into wine. But for that miracle to benefit people, to be more than just a display of divine power, the waiters had to do their job by filling the water jars as He instructed and then distributing the wine. We often talk about trauma surgeons, or firefighters, or hospice nurses, or inner-city school teachers as "doing God's work." That's absolutely true, but it's also true that all of us can do God's work each day in our own jobs, no matter how humble or grand, if we enter into our daily routine with a deep desire to serve God through serving others.

Second, we should seek the intercession of Mary. God acts on His own schedule, as Jesus made clear at Cana when He initially resisted His mother's entreaties by protesting that His time had not yet come. But note how Mary's insistence, driven by her concern for others, combined with the love that Jesus holds for her, moved Him to act at her behest. A major historical and continuing point of dissension between Catholics and our Protestant sisters and brothers is the role we accord the Blessed

Virgin in our theology and prayer. And, truth be told, there have been instances in which well-intentioned Catholic laypeople and even clergy have over-emphasized the role of the Blessed Mother, sometimes at the expense of due attention to God. No doubt Our Lady would be the first to reprove—albeit gently—those who engage in such excesses and to direct them to her son, as she did at Cana. "Do whatever he tells you." That message of the scriptural Mary is also the message of Lourdes and Fatima, where Mary again called us to obedience to the teachings of Jesus and will of God as the paths to earthly peace and eternal salvation.

Third, observe how Jesus solved the servers' problem by refocusing them on something that seemed entirely unrelated, even irrelevant. They had an urgent need for more wine, and He tells them to fill the water jars. Interestingly, those water jars were used for Jewish ceremonial purposes, for washing. How often in the midst of contending with serious problems do we feel that we just don't have time for the "ceremonials"—getting to Mass, praying the Rosary, engaging in the cleansing that comes from the Sacrament of Reconciliation?

The next time our service to others confronts us with challenges, may we have the faith to take our problems to Jesus, through Mary, and to, "Do whatever he tells you," regardless of whether it aligns with our limited sense of what should be done.

For Reflection:

1. What can I do in my current work, whatever it may be, to enable others to benefit from the power of God, following the example of the servants at Cana who filled the water jars at Jesus' command and then distributed the water He turned into wine?

2. When I resent those I serve, to what degree is it fair and appropriate? If my feelings of resentment are misplaced, what thinking do I have to change, what mindset do I have to adopt, to reduce those feelings? If I am right to feel that others are not appreciating, or are taking advantage of, my hard work, what can I do to fix the situation? Do I sometimes indulge others and do their work for them because it contributes to my image as a self-sacrificing person, or gives me a feeling of superiority over them? Do I tolerate other people shifting their work onto me because I'm uncomfortable saying No or am afraid to confront them in a calm but firm manner?

3. Who are the people who serve me and meet my needs whom I don't adequately appreciate? What can I do today to show them due respect and gratitude?

WEDNESDAY, FIRST WEEK OF LENT
NICODEMUS

"Now there was a Pharisee named Nicodemus, a leader of the Jews. He came to Jesus by night and said to him, 'Rabbi, we know that you are a teacher who has come from God; for no one can do these signs that you do apart from the presence of God.' Jesus answered him, 'Very truly, I tell you, no one can see the kingdom of God without being born from above.' Nicodemus said to him, 'How can anyone be born after having grown old? Can one enter a second time into the mother's womb and be born?' Jesus answered, 'Very truly, I tell you, no one can enter the kingdom of God without being born of water and Spirit. What is born of the flesh is flesh, and what is born of the Spirit is spirit. Do not be astonished that I said to you, 'You must be born from above. The wind blows where it chooses, and you hear the sound of it, but you do not know where it comes from or where it goes. So it is with everyone who is born of the Spirit.'

Nicodemus said to him, 'How can these things be?' Jesus answered him, 'Are you a teacher of Israel, and yet you do not understand these things? Very truly, I tell you, we speak of what we know and testify to what we have seen; yet you do not receive our testimony. If I have told you about earthly things and you do not believe, how can you believe if I tell you about heavenly things? No one has ascended into heaven except the one who descended from heaven, the Son of Man. And just as Moses lifted up the serpent in the wilderness, so must the Son of Man be lifted up, that whoever believes in him may have eternal life.' For God so loved the world that he gave his only Son, so that everyone who believes in him may not perish but may have eternal life.' Indeed, God did not send the Son into the world to condemn the world, but in order that the world might be saved through him.'"

John 3:1-17

Nicodemus took a risk in approaching Jesus.

That's why he came to him at night. Nicodemus was a Pharisee and a member of the Sanhedrin, the council of prominent men that had the final say over religious and political questions within the Jewish community. To approach an upstart preacher whose teachings challenged the beliefs of the Pharisees and the power structure of the society was a dangerous act for Nicodemus. It could cost him his position on the Sanhedrin, his reputation in Jerusalem, perhaps more. By every calculation of worldly self-interest and loyalty to his religious tradition, Nicodemus should have stayed as far away from Jesus as possible. Indeed, he should have been at the forefront of those condemning the Nazorean. But he came anyway, albeit furtively, under the cover of darkness.

People in our day still take a risk in approaching Jesus. Faithful Roman Catholics face persecution in China. Christians—particularly recent converts—can experience discrimination, harassment, violence and even death in regions controlled by radical Islamic fundamentalists.

Even here in the United States, approaching Jesus is not without its risks. Consider the modern-day equivalents of Nicodemus, the men and women who rule our business-focused, scientifically driven society not from a Sanhedrin but from corporate boardrooms, research laboratories, media forums, and academic posts. These leaders operate in a world that worships data, dispassionate analysis, and the bottom line. They function in a culture that rejects the notion of enduring, objective right and wrong in favor of discerning nascent trends, no matter how transient, and accommodating consumer preferences, no matter how outlandish or ultimately destructive. To openly embrace Jesus and His teachings in such a society is to risk being portrayed as anything from a quaint anachronism to a bigot or an obstacle to progress.

Those who strive to portray religion and science as implacable antagonists, mutually exclusive means for viewing and living life, will question the intellectual rigor and integrity of the believer. Those who want society to not only tolerate but to actively endorse practices and lifestyles at odds with Catholic teaching will portray the believer as a prude, a fanatic, or some other variety of misanthrope motivated by hate, not love. And those who embrace an economic and social Darwinism, in which productive capacity and profitability are the supreme measures of virtue and value, will dismiss the believer as a sentimentalist lacking the clarity of thinking and strength of will to "make the tough calls."

The risks are real enough, but today as in Nicodemus' time, the greatest risk entailed in approaching Jesus doesn't come from without, but from within. When we approach Jesus, we risk never being the same again. We risk having to acknowledge that all of the illusions and defenses and excuses and consolations and other components of the psychic battlements we have erected to shield us from the reality of our lives are inadequate, and are no substitute for the authenticity that comes from an honest relationship with God. Such authenticity is painful, however, because an honest relationship requires seeing not only the other person for who he or she is, but yourself for who you are. It is impossible to recognize God as the all-powerful, all-loving, perfect Creator without acknowledging that we are the not-all-that-powerful, not-always-loving, quite-imperfect created. And even though we are confronted with the truth of our flawed nature dozens of times in the course of a single day, any suggestion that we are not the be all and end all, and actually are or should be subservient to a higher power, smacks of insult.

It's easier to play it safe. After all, we've invested the best years of our lives in painstakingly constructing our false sense of security. Thank goodness society does its part by telling us that it's all right, whatever *it* may be, and that the answer to any nagging doubt can be found in buying a new car, dropping 15 pounds, making our teeth three shades whiter in just two weeks, having more sex, switching to a better cable service or line of makeup, coloring our hair, and taking a cruise. Make any or all of those changes and you, the essential *you*, won't have to change.

Jesus presents us with a dangerous alternative. Consider the three things he offered Nicodemus. First, Jesus told him how to enter the kingdom of God—by "being born from above." (John 3:3) And showing himself no less intellectually rigorous (and thus dense) than we are today, Nicodemus analyzed the facts and so missed the truth, getting bogged down in literalism rather than opening himself to the profundity of divine revelation. Second, Jesus challenged Nicodemus' knowledge and his grasp of reality: "Are you a teacher of Israel, and yet you do not understand these things?" None of us like to be challenged, particularly in areas where we consider ourselves experts, but unless we're willing to look at life in a radically different way, the life-giving Kingdom right in front of us will remain as invisible as the life-sustaining air all around us. Third, Jesus gave Nicodemus the greatest comfort and measure of true security and love that we can receive, the message of His redemptive mission and how it can save us: "For God so loved the world that he gave his only Son, so that everyone who believes in him may not perish but may have eternal life." (John 3:16)

44

Nicodemus took a risk, and was never the same again. We'll encounter him again, at the end of this narrative, and we'll meet a changed man. The frightened leader who came to Jesus secretly, in the dark, at a time of Jesus' apparent ascent to power, will become the courageous follower who comes to Jesus openly, in the light of day, at a time of Jesus' apparent utter failure.

This Lent, may we take the risk to approach Jesus anew, so that come Easter Sunday, our authentic relationship with the Risen Lord will enable us to never be the same again.

For Reflection:

1. What do I risk in approaching Jesus anew this Lent? What illusions, defenses, excuses, and consolations will I have to discard to see myself as I honestly am and to make room for God to dwell more fully within me and to exercise His healing and saving power?

2. When Nicodemus took the risk of approaching Jesus, he was richly rewarded. How has God rewarded me in my life when I reached out to Him? How can I best draw upon the memory of those blessings to remain in a close, honest relationship with God?

3. How can I support others who have the courage to risk approaching Jesus?

4. How do I want to be changed when Easter arrives? What can I do this Lent to prepare for that lasting change?

THURSDAY, FIRST WEEK OF LENT
THE BAPTIST AND HIS DISCIPLES

"Now a discussion about purification arose between John's disciples and a Jew. They came to John and said to him, 'Rabbi, the one who was with you across the Jordan, to whom you testified, here he is baptizing, and all are going to him.' John answered, 'No one can receive anything except what has been given from heaven. You yourselves are my witnesses that I said, 'I am not the Messiah, but I have been sent ahead of him.' He who has the bride is the bridegroom. The friend of the bridegroom, who stands and hears him, rejoices greatly at the bridegroom's voice. For this reason my joy has been fulfilled. He must increase, but I must decrease.'"
John 3:25-30

This exchange between the Baptist and his followers illustrates the difference between true discipleship and two of its common imitators: religiosity and spiritual egotism.

By this point in the Evangelist's account, John has been preaching his message of repentance for some time. He has encountered Jesus and proclaimed him the Messiah. Jesus has gathered his first disciples and performed the miracle at the wedding feast in Cana. The Lord has driven the money-changers from the temple, and certainly news of this provocative act would have traveled fast and far throughout Jewish society. More profoundly, in the Gospel passage immediately preceding this one, Jesus has begun his teaching, imparting to Nicodemus the words termed by some "The Gospel in Miniature," the words signified by the "John 3:16" signs: "For God so loved the world that he gave his only Son, so that everyone who believes in him may not perish but may have eternal life."

So these devout people, who desired above all else to be good and faithful servants of God, have had the privilege of accompanying the Lord's Herald, and then of actually encountering the Messiah. And what were they worried about? Ceremonial washings.

How myopic. How ridiculous. How like ourselves.

How often do Catholics go to Mass and forget that they are there to worship, not to act as the liturgical equivalent of a movie critic? "When Father Smith elevates the chalice at the consecration, he holds it up with only one hand instead of two." "After Communion, Mrs. Jones stops kneeling and sits back on the pew before the Host has been returned to the Tabernacle and the doors closed." Such keen observers of others' actions rarely consider the more-charitable explanations for minor divergences from what they consider right and proper. For example, perhaps the issues at stake involve orthopedics rather than orthodoxy. Maybe Father Smith has a bum rotator cuff from his days as a high school pitcher, or Mrs. Jones has a terribly arthritic knee. In any event, attention given to such quibbles is attention taken away from the Word of God being proclaimed at Mass, and from the opportunity for communion with God provided by receiving the Body and Blood of Christ. The people of ancient Judea had nothing on us in terms of the ability to miss the presence of God by virtue of a religiosity that focuses on style rather than substance.

Nor is the spiritual egotism of John's disciples unfamiliar to us. The members of John's circle had joined him in the desert and shared his ascetic lifestyle in the hope that this fearless, compelling figure would prove to be the promised one—and that as the people who had been with him from the start, they would enjoy honor and power as his lieutenants. Then

Jesus comes along, and begins attracting more followers and attention. What's worse, rather than challenging this late-comer and putting him in his place, John immediately defers to Him. Those who had sacrificed so much to accompany the Baptist must have been horrified by the thought that perhaps "their man" was not "*the* man."

The Baptist's followers were good people doing good things, but their motives weren't devoid of a measure of ego, just as is the case today. If we're honest, most of us get some ego boost from the leadership role we play on a church committee, or from our service as a lector, or from the sense that we belong to the "dynamic" parish rather than the less-desirable one across town. That doesn't negate the good that we do. And it doesn't mean that we're bad; it just means that we're human.

But whatever part of us is taken up by ego is space unavailable to God as a dwelling place. Hence the persistent admonition down the centuries that Christians must "die to self" if they are to make room for God in their lives. John the Baptist knew this, and tried to teach it to his followers: "He must increase, but I must decrease."

Ours is a society premised on more, not less. The more we have—money, possessions, friends, prestige—the happier we'll be. And even Christians who reject the materialistic component of that proposition still often subscribe to the "more" part: "I need to do more, pray more, care more." That desire isn't necessarily a bad thing, but it can introduce a subtle sort of sacrilege in which we forget that Christ is the savior, not us. It brings us back to the spiritual egotism of what I can do, what I can achieve, what I can make happen. To counter that tendency, Mother Teresa reminded us, "God does not require that we be successful, only that we be faithful."

Lent is a time of less. The sacrifices we choose typically entail less enjoyment of a favorite food, drink, or activity. By not filling ourselves and our days with creature comforts, we create room for the Almighty. But the "less" of Lent isn't only about having fewer things. Let us also work to have fewer worries, fewer wants, fewer plans and priorities. In short, to be "less full of ourselves."

The more we can discard, the more room we make for God. This is the essence of discipleship, because it enables us to follow God's lead. Too often, we expect that it should be the other way around. We expect that God should follow us the way a mother trails after a spoiled child, cleaning up the mess we make of things because we've been guided by our own desires, our own fears, our own sense of how things should be.

And the more we can decrease our ego to increase the space available to God, the easier it is for others to look past our flaws and failings and see God within us. When that happens, when we point others away from ourselves and toward God, we share in the vocation of John the Baptist and in his true discipleship.

For Reflection:

1. When have I been myopic in focusing on small details rather than the big picture in my faith life? How can I change that going forward, and elevate substance over style? In particular, how can I guard against judging others?

2. Are there occasions when I've engaged in spiritual egotism, and been unduly motivated by how people would perceive me and my actions rather than by the intrinsic value of those actions?

3. What things within me am I most unwilling to decrease to make more room for God? What can I learn about myself from identifying these things, and how should I respond to what I've learned about myself?

4. How can I interact with others in a way that shows them more of God and less of me?

FRIDAY, FIRST WEEK OF LENT
THE SAMARITAN WOMAN

"But he had to go through Samaria. So he came to a Samaritan city called
Sychar, near the plot of ground that Jacob had given to his son Joseph.
Jacob's well was there, and Jesus, tired out by his journey, was sitting by
the well. It was about noon.

A Samaritan woman came to draw water, and Jesus said to her, 'Give me
a drink.' (His disciples had gone to the city to buy food.) The Samaritan
woman said to him, 'How is it that you, a Jew, ask a drink of me, a
woman of Samaria?' (Jews do not share things in common with
Samaritans.) Jesus answered her, 'If you knew the gift of God, and who it
is that is saying to you, 'Give me a drink,' you would have asked him,
and he would have given you living water.' The woman said to him, 'Sir,
you have no bucket, and the well is deep. Where do you get that living
water? Are you greater than our ancestor Jacob, who gave us the well, and
with his sons and his flocks drank from it?' Jesus said to her, 'Everyone
who drinks of this water will be thirsty again, but those who drink of the
water that I will give them will never be thirsty. The water that I will give
will become in them a spring of water gushing up to eternal life.' The
woman said to him, 'Sir, give me this water, so that I may never be thirsty
or have to keep coming here to draw water.'

Jesus said to her, 'Go, call your husband, and come back.' The woman
answered him, 'I have no husband.' Jesus said to her, 'You are right in
saying, 'I have no husband'; for you have had five husbands, and the one
you have now is not your husband. What you have said is true!' The
woman said to him, 'Sir, I see that you are a prophet. Our ancestors
worshiped on this mountain, but you say that the place where people must
worship is in Jerusalem.' Jesus said to her, 'Woman, believe me, the hour
is coming when you will worship the Father neither on this mountain nor
in Jerusalem. You worship what you do not know; we worship what we
know, for salvation is from the Jews. But the hour is coming, and is now

here, when the true worshipers will worship the Father in spirit and truth, for the Father seeks such as these to worship him. God is spirit, and those who worship him must worship in spirit and truth.' The woman said to him, 'I know that Messiah is coming' (who is called Christ). 'When he comes, he will proclaim all things to us.' Jesus said to her, 'I am he, the one who is speaking to you.'

Just then his disciples came. They were astonished that he was speaking with a woman, but no one said, 'What do you want?' or, 'Why are you speaking with her?' Then the woman left her water jar and went back to the city. She said to the people, 'Come and see a man who told me everything I have ever done! He cannot be the Messiah, can he?' They left the city and were on their way to him. Meanwhile the disciples were urging him, 'Rabbi, eat something.' But he said to them, 'I have food to eat that you do not know about.' So the disciples said to one another, 'Surely no one has brought him something to eat?'

Jesus said to them, 'My food is to do the will of him who sent me and to complete his work. Do you not say, 'Four months more, then comes the harvest'? But I tell you, look around you, and see how the fields are ripe for harvesting. The reaper is already receiving wages and is gathering fruit for eternal life, so that sower and reaper may rejoice together. For here the saying holds true, 'One sows and another reaps.' I sent you to reap that for which you did not labor. Others have labored, and you have entered into their labor.'

Many Samaritans from that city believed in him because of the woman's testimony, 'He told me everything I have ever done.' So when the Samaritans came to him, they asked him to stay with them; and he stayed there two days. And many more believed because of his word. They said to the woman, 'It is no longer because of what you said that we believe, for we have heard for ourselves, and we know that this is truly the Savior of the world.'"
John 4:4-42

A Samaritan woman living with a man to whom she was not married.

Short of the woman also having leprosy, it would be difficult to describe a person further removed from the standards of respectability and acceptability in the society in which Jesus lived.

The fact that the Lord revealed himself as the Messiah to this woman and selected her to bring others to Him speaks volumes about how God works, and about how much we can do for God whatever our faults, failings, or place in society. To appreciate all that this Gospel passage has to offer, however, let's step back from that overarching truth for a moment and consider the details of the account.

We'll start with how the woman came to encounter Jesus. She went to the well to draw water, to meet one of the basic needs of life. As she was working to meet her needs, however, God asked her to meet His. So often as we pursue our fundamental needs—for love and acceptance, for employment and financial security, for physical health and peace of mind— God asks us to help answer the prayers of others whose needs are far greater than ours. Maybe this means helping a person at work who is struggling to get a handle on a challenging assignment, or adding a few items for the community food bank to your shopping cart at the supermarket. Perhaps it means that you spend your time in the doctor's waiting room talking with the person nearby whose pallor and gaunt frame signify grave illness. Whatever the case, in the course of pursuing what we need, there is no shortage of opportunities to help others in need.

Next, there's the issue of what the woman wanted and what Jesus offered her instead. After she heard the Lord's promise to provide water that would become "a spring of water gushing up to eternal life," the woman replies, "Sir, give me this water, so that I may never be thirsty or have to keep coming here to draw water." (John 4:14-15) Like the Samaritan woman, we are offered the incredible gift of everlasting life and we say, in effect, "That's great, but what I really need is for things to be better for me here and now." Just as the woman asked God's help so that she wouldn't have to keep trekking to the well every day and carrying a heavy bucket back home, we want God to relieve us of our ongoing search for the right person, the right job, the right diagnosis and treatment. If we didn't want these things, we wouldn't be human, and if we didn't turn to God to meet our temporal needs, we wouldn't be faithful Christians. But when we don't get what we want in this life, it's important to remember that what God ultimately will provide for us if we believe in Him far surpasses anything that may or may not work out as we would wish here.

This brings us to the point in the account where Jesus asks the woman to go and get her husband. As their subsequent exchange makes clear, Jesus knew perfectly well that the man with whom the woman was living was not her husband. The Lord was giving the woman a chance to tell the truth, to be honest with Him. And she did just that, even though it didn't reflect well on her. In return for that honesty, that acknowledgment of her sinfulness and shortcomings, Jesus revealed to her what His Father wanted—for people to worship Him in Spirit and truth—and even revealed to her that He was the Messiah. God, who knows everything, doesn't need us to tell Him about our faults and failings. *We*, however, do need to acknowledge our sinfulness to rid ourselves of the notion that we can "go it alone" or "don't need anyone to help us." Seeing ourselves as we truly are gives us the clarity and focus to see God as He truly is, and to ask His forgiveness and accept His love.

The disciples return immediately after Jesus has told the woman that He is the Messiah, and while they don't come out and ask the Lord why he was talking with her, they clearly are wondering about it. To their credit, they are genuinely intent on serving Jesus, urging Him to eat the food they have brought Him, and are upset when He declines their offer. "Good, church-going Catholics" can become upset when God seems to be using someone else, someone not up to our standards of respectability, to do His work. At such times, we would do well to remember how Jesus asked the Samaritan woman, not his disciples, to provide for His needs, and to bear in mind the Lord's admonition that in the end any good that we are able to do on His behalf represents reaping what others have sowed.

Finally, let's consider how the Samaritan woman served as a means for the Lord's ends. After her encounter with Jesus at the well, she could have gone back to town and tried to evangelize from a position of spiritual superiority: "*I* just met the Messiah! He asked *me* for a drink. He revealed His identity to *me*. He chose *me* to carry this message." Instead, to convince her fellow townspeople that Jesus was sent from God, she twice said that He had "told me everything I have ever done." (John 4:29 and 4:39) Her reputation must have been well-known in the small town, and her neighbors had to have understood what she meant by this statement. So, in seeking to lead people to Jesus, she started from a position of humility, readily acknowledging her own sinfulness as a means of causing people to believe in Jesus and to come to meet Him. May this lesson, and the others to be found in Jesus' encounter with the Samaritan woman, remain with us throughout this Lent and beyond.

For Reflection:

1. As I "go to the well" to meet my basic, everyday needs, how can I find ways to help others whose needs are greater than mine?

2. How can I bear in mind that what Jesus offers me isn't necessarily comfort and success in this world, but eternal life? How can I use that realization to shape my wants and temper my disappointments?

3. Am I sometimes "spiritually conceited"? How can I approach God and others from a starting point of humility and acknowledgment of my faults and failings?

4. The Psalmist tells us that "If today you hear his voice, harden not your hearts." How can I listen to others in a way that allows me to hear the voice of God in people, like the Samaritan woman, who I normally would not expect to be speaking on behalf of the Most High? How can I guard against hardening my heart so that I am able to hear God in all the ways and through all the people by which He speaks to me?

SATURDAY, FIRST WEEK OF LENT
THE ROYAL OFFICIAL

"Now there was a royal official whose son lay ill in Capernaum. When he heard that Jesus had come from Judea to Galilee, he went and begged him to come down and heal his son, for he was at the point of death. Then Jesus said to him, 'Unless you see signs and wonders you will not believe.' The official said to him, 'Sir, come down before my little boy dies.' Jesus said to him, 'Go; your son will live.' The man believed the word that Jesus spoke to him and started on his way. As he was going down, his slaves met him and told him that his child was alive. So he asked them the hour when he began to recover, and they said to him, 'Yesterday at one in the afternoon the fever left him.' The father realized that this was the hour when Jesus had said to him, 'Your son will live.' So he himself believed, along with his whole household."

John 4:46-53

Being a royal official means knowing who's who and what's what.

You understand the chain of command and the distribution of power. You devote much of your time to calculating how to shuffle your priorities and shift your allegiances, what to emphasize and what to play down, who to flatter and who to spurn, in keeping with evolving developments. Maintaining your power base, burnishing your reputation, winning promotion all require exquisite attention to the subtlest signs and earliest indicators of change. In modern parlance, it's called "situational awareness," and the most successful politicians and celebrities, Wall Street traders and corporate raiders, possess the quality to an almost preternatural degree.

Being a parent, meanwhile, means knowing there is nothing you won't do to help a gravely ill son or daughter.

You understand the fear of loss and the desperation and determination that drive your pursuit of a cure. You devote your time to investigating treatment options, finding experts, hoping and searching for some research break-through or alternative approach. It's called "unbounded love," and in recent years movies including "Lorenzo's Oil" and "My Sister's Keeper" have documented the extraordinary lengths to which parents will go to try to save a child facing death. Our own circle of family and friends almost certainly provides similar stories as heroic and heart-wrenching.

Being a royal official (or corporate executive, or mid-level manager, or small business owner, or construction-trades worker, or anyone else) _and_ the parent of a gravely ill child means knowing you have to decide what comes first.

For the royal official in John's Gospel, the choice before him was no choice at all. The man accustomed to carefully considering his priorities cast everything else aside in an attempt to save his son. The man used to summoning others to his presence hastened out to find Jesus. The man keenly aware of protocol and pecking order, who regularly had others begging him for favors, could have cared less about standing on ceremony or demonstrating his importance, and without the least pomp implored Jesus to help his son.

Approaching this itinerant rabbi whose aims and teachings were deemed highly suspect by the authorities meant disregarding, even rejecting, the power structure to which he had given his allegiance and depended on for his current position and any hope of advancement. But none of that mattered compared to the hope of saving his child.

If, God forbid, we found ourselves in his situation, no doubt we would do the same thing. There's no question of our love for our children, spouses, siblings, and closest friends. There is perhaps, however, a question of how we set our priorities and balance our lives in the less dramatic and dire circumstances that, thankfully, are the norm for most of us.

You don't have to be a royal official, or Senate candidate or pop star or hedge fund manager, to feel the demands of your occupation, the pressure to continually demonstrate your value. Your company didn't win the bid for that big job it was counting on, and there's talk of layoffs. The new boss is going to make her mark by shaking things up, and she seems to be taking a close look at everyone's performance. There are rumors of a buyout, or of shifting jobs to another part of the country—or world—where labor costs are lower.

We can't ignore the responsibilities and realities of the workplace. We would do ourselves and our families a disservice if we didn't put in the hours and the effort necessary to do our jobs well. It's important that we recognize and respond to opportunities that can lead to greater success, higher earnings, a promotion. We can't be blind to potential threats on the horizon. And, sadly, we know that sometimes performance and merit aren't always enough, and that a bit of politicking might also be required.

But we also know that time accelerates as each year goes by. The career will be over and the house will be empty all too soon. We know that every person, every family, however blessed for however long, will face tragedy or devastating news of some sort.

Against that eventuality, we want to cultivate the faith of the royal official, but we don't want to emulate his timing. We don't want to wait until a crisis is upon us to approach the Lord, to put our trust in Him and, in the process, to acknowledge that our allegiance to Him trumps our loyalty to anything else.

The Gospel account tells us that after Jesus assured the royal official that his son would live, the man returned home and was greeted upon his arrival with the wonderful news that the boy was recovering. John explains that he then asked his servants when the child began to get better, and:

> "They said to him, 'Yesterday at one in the afternoon the fever left him.' The father realized that this was the hour when Jesus had said to him, 'Your son will live.' So he himself believed, along with his whole household." (John 4:52-53)

We can become fevered in meeting our obligations, striving for a bigger bonus or higher title, mulling the machinations of the workplace. Solid effort, healthy ambition, and a heads-up approach can slide into obsession in a way that warps priorities and elevates means into ends.

We can be cured of that illness by coming to Jesus with all of our fears and hopes and requests. Our recovery can begin, as it did for the royal official's son, the moment we place our trust in Him. Our allegiance is clarified, our priorities put in proper order, our faith rewarded—our fever broken and our spiritual and emotional health restored. And our wellness can be contagious. Like the royal official transformed by his encounter with Jesus, we can return to our homes and families and conduct ourselves in a way that will prompt others to say that because of us our "whole household" came to believe."

For Reflection:

1. What priorities, allegiances, and concerns have taken on undue importance in my life? In what cases have "means," such as work that provides materially for my family and me and rewards me with a healthy sense of accomplishment, become "ends" unto themselves? This Lent, how can I begin to re-order my priorities in a practical way that puts God and loved ones first while still enabling me to honor my commitments and fulfill my obligations to my employer and others?

2. In moments of crisis, such as that faced by the royal official, have I turned to God as quickly and with as much faith as that man did? This Lent, how can I develop the habit of bringing all things to God, good and bad, and putting matters in His hands with utter trust in His love for me?

3. How can I bring the people in my life to faith (or deeper faith) in Jesus by the example I set with my actions and priorities?

MONDAY, SECOND WEEK OF LENT
THE SICK MAN AT BETHESDA

"Now in Jerusalem by the Sheep Gate there is a pool, called in Hebrew Beth-zatha, which has five porticoes. In these lay many invalids—blind, lame, and paralyzed. One man was there who had been ill for thirty-eight years. When Jesus saw him lying there and knew that he had been there a long time, he said to him, 'Do you want to be made well?' The sick man answered him, 'Sir, I have no one to put me into the pool when the water is stirred up; and while I am making my way, someone else steps down ahead of me.' Jesus said to him, 'Stand up, take your mat and walk.' At once the man was made well, and he took up his mat and began to walk.

Now that day was a sabbath. So the Jews said to the man who had been cured, 'It is the sabbath; it is not lawful for you to carry your mat.' But he answered them, 'The man who made me well said to me, 'Take up your mat and walk.' " They asked him, 'Who is the man who said to you, 'Take it up and walk'?' ¹³ Now the man who had been healed did not know who it was, for Jesus had disappeared in the crowd that was there. Later Jesus found him in the temple and said to him, 'See, you have been made well! Do not sin anymore, so that nothing worse happens to you.' The man went away and told the Jews that it was Jesus who had made him well."
John 5:2-15

Jesus asks us the same question he asked the sick man at Bethesda: Do you want to be made well?

It isn't a trick question, but sometimes we reply with a "trick answer."

Of course we want to be well; who doesn't? That's the obvious answer, the easy answer, but there's often a more complicated component to our response lurking behind our spoken words.

No matter how much we may complain that we're "stuck," consigned like the sick man at Bethesda to sit still while we watch the world go by, there's a certain security in our sedentary plight. The chair in which we count the hours until 5 p.m. in our job, the couch on which we pass our nights in front of the television, or the bar stool on which we drown our sorrows provides a familiar vantage point from which to view all that is happening around us. It's as good a spot as any to wait for someone or something to come along, pick us up, and carry us to a place of restoration. We're not far from what we want and need, just as the man Jesus approached was only a few steps from the healing waters. All that man required was for something to stir up those waters and then someone to get him into the pool. All we require is for someone to stir things up for us and then help us take the plunge. And yet, things never quite work out. The timing isn't right. No one is there to help at the critical moment. Somebody else always gets there first.

The Evangelist tells us that even before He approached the man lying on his mat, Jesus knew that the man had been ill for many years. The Lord knows how long we have borne our suffering, and He knows the exact nature of our spiritual infirmities.

He comes to us this Lent fully aware of how often people haven't been there for us when we needed them. And He tells us, stop looking to anyone other than me; stop waiting for the time to be right. In keeping with the inspired words of Isaiah, He says:

> "In a time of favor I have answered you, on a day of salvation I have helped you." (Isaiah 49:8)

66

Or, more plainly, "Stand up, take your mat and walk." The man at Bethesda did just that. He didn't question, plan, or protest. He got up and got moving.

But it can't be that easy.

Actually, we don't know how easy it was or wasn't. The Evangelist doesn't tell us whether the man strode away at a brisk pace, or whether his initial steps were faltering, his gait unsteady for the first few minutes or hours or days. But we do know that the man walked. And we also know that sometimes we're the ones who make moving on harder than it has to be.

J. Patrick Kelly, OFM, PhD, is a priest of the Order of Friars Minor and a very wise and accomplished psychotherapist. For more than 30 years he counseled people contending with emotional problems. The Franciscan tells how patients often would prevent themselves from recognizing readily apparent realities because identifying a problem makes it possible to begin the difficult, painful task of addressing that problem.

As Father Kelly tells it, it was not uncommon for a new patient to open a dialogue with him that unfolded something like this:

"I really hope you can help me, Father. I'm terribly unhappy."

"I'm very sorry to hear that. What is making you so unhappy?"

"I don't know, Father."

"Well, what do you think it might be?"

"I just don't know," said with an edge of defensiveness creeping into the patient's voice. "I've racked my brain, and thought and thought, and I just can't figure it out."

Having been down this road many times before, the priest-therapist would pause, and then ask a question, introduced with a touch of validation and empathy, that had an uncanny ability to get to the heart of the matter.

"I understand that you don't know, and I appreciate how difficult it can be to unravel these things. But tell me something. If you *did* know what the problem was, what would it be?"

At that point, like floodwaters bursting through a dam, a patient often would blurt out, "My marriage is falling apart," or, "I have a drinking problem that is ruining my life," or, "I feel like I'm a total failure."

And then the healing could begin.

We know, at some deep level, what our problems are. The Lord knows them, too. And this Lent, He calls us to not let them paralyze us, to not let them keep us stuck in a place where we are so conscious of our inadequacies and imperfections that we find it safer to sit still and wait for some ideal time, some other person, to come along and make things right. Instead, He says, in essence, You and I will do this together. My grace and your trust in Me can make this your appointed time, your acceptable hour, your time of favor.

If we accept that invitation this Lent, we may find ourselves—at least initially—in a landscape as unfamiliar as the desert in which Jesus dwelt during His forty days of preparation for His public ministry. (Matthew 4:1-11) And we can expect some around us to challenge and criticize what we're doing, just as many who should have rejoiced at the sick man's recovery instead chose to rebuke him for carrying his mat on the sabbath. But however imperfectly and uncertainly, we will be moving, not sitting still. Our steps will lead us toward wholeness, and thus holiness. And in making that journey, we will help bring others to the Lord, because we will be able to emulate the faithful man of Bethesda who gratefully proclaimed "that it was Jesus who had made him well." (John 5:15)

For Reflection:

1. Are there aspects of my life where I'm "stuck"? If so, where would I rather be, and what's holding me back from moving in that direction? Am I getting any benefits, or avoiding any risks, by sitting still?

2. Do I ever look to others to do things for me that I should be doing for myself? If so, how can I use this Lent to take a more independent and faith-filled approach to acting on my own behalf?

3. Do I tend to resist taking steps unless the timing is exactly right or until I feel I can do something perfectly? How much has that attitude precluded me from doing and experiencing? How can I live my life more fully by accepting my imperfections and trusting God to supply what I will need to grow and move forward?

TUESDAY, SECOND WEEK OF LENT
THE BOY WITH THE
LOAVES AND FISHES

"After this Jesus went to the other side of the Sea of Galilee, also called the Sea of Tiberias. A large crowd kept following him, because they saw the signs that he was doing for the sick. Jesus went up the mountain and sat down there with his disciples. Now the Passover, the festival of the Jews, was near. When he looked up and saw a large crowd coming toward him, Jesus said to Philip, 'Where are we to buy bread for these people to eat?' He said this to test him, for he himself knew what he was going to do. Philip answered him, 'Six months' wages would not buy enough bread for each of them to get a little.' One of his disciples, Andrew, Simon Peter's brother, said to him, 'There is a boy here who has five barley loaves and two fish. But what are they among so many people?' Jesus said, 'Make the people sit down.' Now there was a great deal of grass in the place; so they sat down, about five thousand in all. Then Jesus took the loaves, and when he had given thanks, he distributed them to those who were seated; so also the fish, as much as they wanted. When they were satisfied, he told his disciples, 'Gather up the fragments left over, so that nothing may be lost.' So they gathered them up, and from the fragments of the five barley loaves, left by those who had eaten, they filled twelve baskets."

John 6:1-13

The "miracle of the loaves and fishes" or the "feeding of the 5,000" recounted in this Gospel passage has become a cause of theological contention. At issue is the question of exactly *how* Jesus fed the multitudes. The traditional view is that the Lord exercised direct, divine action to perform a miracle, just as he did in turning the water to wine at the wedding feast in Cana. More recently, however, some theologians have proposed that what actually happened is that the teachings of Jesus

71

prompted people to share with others the food they had brought with them for personal sustenance, and that the ability to feed the whole crowd and still have a surplus of bread shows what can be accomplished when the Gospel message moves people from selfishness to generosity.

It can be intriguing, at least initially, to mull over such questions. Given their unfathomable nature, however, we're probably best served moving along sooner rather than later, secure in the knowledge that neither we nor the world's most eminent theologians are going to have a definitive answer this side of glory and, more importantly, that the answer has zero impact on making us better people and more-faithful Christians.

Fortunately, the "miracle of the loaves and fishes"—the only miracle other than the Lord's Resurrection to be cited in all four Gospels—provides clear direction on two intertwined issues far more germane to the contemporary Christian life.

The first concerns the limitations of our own resources. As the Gospel notes, Jesus was testing Philip when he looked out at the multitudes and asked, "Where are we to buy bread for these people to eat?" We, too, are tested by this question. Where—and how—can we acquire enough to satisfy our hunger, to feed the multitude of needs within us?

Ultimately, no matter how wealthy we may be, how talented and capable we may be, we have to respond with the answer that Philip gave Jesus: We don't possess the resources required to meet all of our needs.

Remember, as the Evangelist tells us, Jesus already knew what He was going to do, how He was going to intervene to overcome the inability of the disciples to feed all the people, but

He posed the question to enable Philip to understand and acknowledge the limitations of human effort.

God already knows what we need and how He will provide it to us, but until we acknowledge our own limitations and let Him come to our aid, we will struggle as fruitlessly—and dangerously—as a person choking in a restaurant who refuses other diners' efforts to save him by wrapping their arms around him and performing the Heimlich maneuver.

We can spend a lot of time thrashing about when confronted with our inability to meet our own needs. Note, however, the instructions Jesus gave for the hungry crowds that had followed Him. He didn't say that people should start foraging for food, or build fires for cooking, or make for the nearest town and its inns. Rather, he said, "Make the people sit down." There are times, such as we read about and reflected on yesterday in the account of the sick man at Bethesda, when God calls us to action. At other points, however, He calls us to sit still and let Him do the work. The people whom the Lord fed that day were His *followers* in the most literal sense of the word; the Evangelist tells us that when Jesus crossed the Sea of Galilee, "a large crowd kept *following* him." So first we have to move -- our lives, our hearts, our outlook—so that we bring ourselves as close to Jesus as we're able. Then, we have to count on Him to satisfy our hunger, trusting in His promise that, "I am the bread of life. Whoever comes to me will never be hungry, and whoever believes in me will never be thirsty." (John 6:35)

If the first lesson Jesus taught his disciples concerned the limitations of human endeavor in and of itself, the second that He imparted is that even the most meager human effort, when assisted by God, can be sufficient to overcome any difficulty.

73

You can almost hear the plaintive tone in Andrew's voice and see him shrugging his shoulders when he tells the Lord, "There is a boy here who has five barley loaves and two fish. But what are they among so many people?"

Contrast that sense of futility with the boy's attitude. He saw a need and he responded by offering everything he possessed. Had he been prudent, he would have kept the loaves and fish for himself. Had he been calculating, he would have kept a bit for himself and sold the rest at an exorbitant price. Had he been as "practical" as Andrew, he would have seen there was no point in offering his resources for the common good. Thankfully, the boy was imprudent, unselfish, and impractical, and so provided the inadequate human offering that the Lord blessed and transformed into an overabundance of supply.

What Jesus taught His followers on the mountainside that day, and what He continues to teach us, is that we need God if our efforts are to succeed and that God needs us—in a certain sense—to help build His kingdom on earth.

As St. Teresa of Avila, the 16th Century mystic and Doctor of the Church, wrote from her Carmelite convent almost 500 years ago:

> Christ has no body but yours,
>
> No hands, no feet on earth but yours,
>
> Yours are the eyes with which he looks
>
> Compassion on this world.
>
> Yours are the feet with which he walks to do good,
>
> Yours are the hands with which he blesses all the world.

So our job is to make the effort, no matter how inadequate, inept, or unequal to the task we may feel. If what we're trying to accomplish accords with God's will, His blessing will more than suffice to assure its success.

For Reflection:

1. What needs or hungers have I been unable to satisfy on my own? How can I follow the example of the multitudes who reclined at the Lord's direction and "sit still" long enough for God to work with the meager resources I offer Him? Which of those unmet needs are healthy ones, and will contribute to my well-being, and which perhaps remain unmet because they are not in my best interests?

2. Have there been times when I took shelter behind my sense of inadequacy as an excuse to avoid taking on an important task?

3. Considering the causes and social needs that matter most to me, how can I join with others and ask God's aid so that my own work and talents can contribute to a larger effort to achieve a worthwhile goal?

WEDNESDAY, SECOND WEEK OF LENT
THE DISCIPLES WHO TURNED BACK

"So Jesus said to them, 'Very truly, I tell you, unless you eat the flesh of the Son of Man and drink his blood, you have no life in you. Those who eat my flesh and drink my blood have eternal life, and I will raise them up on the last day; for my flesh is true food and my blood is true drink. Those who eat my flesh and drink my blood abide in me, and I in them. Just as the living Father sent me, and I live because of the Father, so whoever eats me will live because of me. This is the bread that came down from heaven, not like that which your ancestors ate, and they died. But the one who eats this bread will live forever.' He said these things while he was teaching in the synagogue at Capernaum. When many of his disciples heard it, they said, 'This teaching is difficult; who can accept it?' But Jesus, being aware that his disciples were complaining about it, said to them, 'Does this offend you? Then what if you were to see the Son of Man ascending to where he was before? It is the spirit that gives life; the flesh is useless. The words that I have spoken to you are spirit and life. But among you there are some who do not believe.' For Jesus knew from the first who were the ones that did not believe, and who was the one that would betray him. And he said, 'For this reason I have told you that no one can come to me unless it is granted by the Father.' Because of this many of his disciples turned back and no longer went about with him."

John 6:53-66

Remember the phrase "shock and awe"?

In January 1991, the United States and its allies launched their offensive to drive Iraqi troops out of Kuwait with a massive aerial bombardment that decimated Saddam Hussein's command and control centers. The Pentagon explained that the goal was to induce "shock and awe" to break the Iraqis' will and ability to resist the ground attacks that followed.

On its face, it would seem highly inappropriate, almost blasphemous, to draw upon a military campaign and the death and destruction it entails to speak to the work of God and our response. But the phrase "shock and awe" has uncommon value in describing the effect of the Almighty's intervention in human history in the person of Jesus and, hopefully, the way in which we greet that tremendous act of mercy and love.

So much about Jesus was shocking. He was conceived by an unmarried woman. He consorted with tax collectors, publicans, and prostitutes. He challenged the religious conventions and authorities of His time. And He did and said and taught outrageous things, as we read in this passage.

At this point in John's Gospel, the Lord has changed water into wine at the wedding feast in Cana, cured people, and performed the miracle of the loaves and fishes. As news of these deeds spread, a huge crowd began following Him. They were hanging on His every word to see if Jesus would reveal himself as the Messiah. But when they heard what He had to say, when He offered them the way to eternal life, they didn't rejoice; they recoiled.

"This saying is difficult; who can accept it?" they asked. (John 7:60) So many people ask the same thing today. Many of our Protestant brothers and sisters insist upon a literal reading of the Bible when it comes to the creation narrative in Genesis, but have a new-found appreciation for the role of allegory in Scripture when faced with these words spoken by Christ Himself.

Even many Catholics reject the doctrine of transubstantiation. In February 2008, Georgetown University's Center for Applied Research in the Apostolate (CARA) surveyed 1,007 adults in the United States who identified themselves as

Catholics. The survey found that among those who reported attending Mass weekly, 91 percent reported believing that Jesus is really present in the Eucharist. That proportion fell to roughly two-thirds of those who reported they don't attend Mass each week but do attend at least once a month, and to just 40 percent of those who said they go to Mass a few times a year or less.*

A subsequent survey by *National Catholic Reporter* suggests that the first step in convincing many Catholics about the Real Presence is *informing* them of the Real Presence. In 2011, the publication surveyed 1,442 U.S. adults who identified themselves as Catholics. Those people were asked:

> "Which of the following statements best describes the Catholic teaching about the bread and wine used for communion?
>
> 1. The bread and wine become the body and blood of Jesus Christ.
>
> 2. The bread and wine are only symbols of the body and blood of Jesus Christ.

Half of the respondents chose the latter answer, saying that to their knowledge, the Church teaches that the bread and wine are only symbols.

This sad percentage speaks poorly of our catechetical efforts, but a related finding speaks wonderfully of God's ability to place in the heart what we fail to communicate to the mind. Roughly one in three of those who said they did not know that the Church teaches that upon consecration the bread and wine

---

* http://cara.georgetown.edu/sacraments.html

really become the body of blood of Christ said that they believed this doctrine even though they had not been taught it!*

These faithful people, termed "unknowing believers" by *National Catholic Reporter*, are a sign of great hope, and of God's sufficiency in the face of our own inadequacy. They are the opposite of the discouraged disciples whom John describes. Those disciples heard about the reality of the Bread of Life from the one who is the Bread of Life, and chose not to believe. The so-called "unknowing believers" apparently haven't had the benefit of even a CCD teacher explaining this doctrine to them, much less hearing it directly from the Lord during His time on earth, and yet they have heeded some stirring of the spirit within and embraced this profound reality.

In fairness to the doubters of Jesus' times, the idea *is* shocking. Even today, if you were to talk to someone with absolutely no knowledge of Christ or Christianity and explain that when the priests says the words of consecration at Mass, the bread and wine truly become flesh and blood that then are consumed by the faithful, the person would likely find the idea fantastical and grotesque. But we have an advantage over those who departed from Jesus at that point of His ministry, and over those today who know nothing of Christ. We know how the story of Jesus' time on earth began—and we know how it ended.

And that brings us back to shock and awe. Conceived by a teenaged virgin. Shocking. Preferred the company of society's outcasts to respectable authorities. Shocking. Challenged the conventions of His time, and when that behavior

---

* http:ncronline.org/print/news/catholics-america/knowledge-and-belief-about-real-presence

put His life in peril, refused the opportunity to dodge a horrific death. Shocking. Rose from the dead. Shocking.

If we believe all of that, how difficult is it to believe that the Lord who in His love came to us, taught us, suffered for us, died for us, and rose for us, would have both the desire and the ability to continue to come to us in the Eucharist?

This Lent, and always, may our shock inspire the awe that not only makes us come to the Eucharist with profound reverence, but that also sends us forth with the bold faith needed to bring others to accept the real truth of the Real Presence.

For Reflection:

1. Are there times when I have been a "discouraged disciple" and found it difficult to accept the truth of the Real Presence? What contributed to those doubts, and how did I—or can I now—best allay them?

2. Does the way in which I approach the Eucharist—spiritually and physically—reflect my belief in the Real Presence and the awe and reverence it should inspire?

3. When was the last time I took advantage of the opportunity to spend quiet time with the Lord at Eucharistic Adoration, or just by praying in a silent Church while the Body of Christ was reserved in the tabernacle?

4. How, through my actions and words, can I in a loving, patient way bring others around me to know and accept the Real Presence of Christ in the Eucharist and help them come to receive and benefit from the graces the Eucharist offers?

THURSDAY, SECOND WEEK OF LENT
THE ACCUSERS OF THE WOMAN CAUGHT IN ADULTERY

"Early in the morning he came again to the temple. All the people came to him and he sat down and began to teach them. The scribes and the Pharisees brought a woman who had been caught in adultery; and making her stand before all of them, they said to him, 'Teacher, this woman was caught in the very act of committing adultery. Now in the law Moses commanded us to stone such women. Now what do you say?' They said this to test him, so that they might have some charge to bring against him. Jesus bent down and wrote with his finger on the ground. When they kept on questioning him, he straightened up and said to them, 'Let anyone among you who is without sin be the first to throw a stone at her.' And once again he bent down and wrote on the ground. When they heard it, they went away, one by one, beginning with the elders; and Jesus was left alone with the woman standing before him."

John 8:2-9

The scribes and the Pharisees were smart men.

They knew an opportunity when they saw one, and in this hapless woman "caught in the act," they recognized the chance they had been seeking to present Jesus with an untenable choice. If He endorsed the ancient commandment and agreed that the woman should be stoned to death, many of His followers would recoil from that brutality, and would no longer view Him as someone different, someone special. If, on the other hand, He called for mercy, Jesus would be breaking with the Law and the Prophets, and they would have the proof they needed to bring charges against Him.

It was quite the trap, and if the woman lost her life because they had used her as bait, it was a small price to pay. After all, she was a criminal by the laws of their society, and they had to protect their positions against a challenger who threatened to up-end the whole power structure.

We don't know the circumstances of the assignation that put this woman's life in peril. We don't know whether she was in a loving, albeit illicit, relationship, or whether her partner had paid her for sex, or perhaps even had coerced her into sex. (Interesting, isn't it, that while the woman is publicly humiliated and faces a horrific death, there's no mention of the man incurring any punishment?) What we can be sure of, however, is that even if her partner had no feelings for her and was actuated by nothing more than lust, the scribes and Pharisees took advantage of this poor woman much more callously than any scheming seducer could have.

Flash forward to our own "zero-tolerance" society.

Elected officials eager to demonstrate that they are "tough on crime" pass mandatory-sentencing measures that fill our jails and prisons with many people whose core offense is being addicted to drugs or mentally ill or too poor to afford adequate legal representation. At least 27 states have enacted "three strikes and you're out" laws that require long— sometimes *life*-long—sentences for people convicted of three crimes. In some states, relatively minor and non-violent offenses can count toward one or even two of the three strikes.

Crime should be punished, of course, and the fact that a mugger is mentally ill or a burglar addicted to heroin doesn't in any way lessen the trauma and loss experienced by their victims. But regardless of whether you think these offenders' motivations should or should not be a consideration in their

84

sentencing, the motivation of those who mandate the sentences certainly merits examination.

Many a candidate has won election by railing not only against crime, but also against the supposedly "soft" judges who "coddle felons." These lawmakers are the epitome of righteous indignation, and when it comes to the circumstances that might have led a defendant down the wrong path, they "don't want to hear it."

Until, that is, they find themselves standing before a judge. Then it's all about context and perspective, and weighing years of devoted public service against one aberrant act, and defenses involving Twinkies and other causes that beggar belief. In this respect, our elected officials are faithful representatives of their constituents. We, too, want to see the law strictly enforced—until we drive up to the police checkpoint "that one night" when we lingered at the restaurant for an after-dinner drink instead of calling it quits after our customary two glasses of wine. We have no sympathy for juvenile delinquents—until we get the call to come down to the station to pick up our teenager, "a good kid who was just in the wrong place at the wrong time."

The modern-day lawmakers who espouse a "lock them up and throw away the key" philosophy to win re-election are kindred spirits with the scribes and Pharisees who dragged the woman before Jesus. Like our headline-craving politicians, the scribes and Pharisees weren't motivated primarily, if at all, by a desire to see justice done. They were threatened by Jesus and the fact that more and more people were coming to hear His teaching. So the hapless woman became a means to their own end.

Jesus, however, has a disconcerting habit of directing what we would ask of or wish for others back to ourselves. When He gave us the Lord's Prayer, Jesus taught us to ask the Father to forgive us to the same extent that we forgive those who trespass against us. If we're honest about our own capacity and willingness to forgive, that's a frightening prospect. The scribes and Pharisees must have been similarly abashed when, rather than choosing between the unacceptable choices they gave Him, the Lord turned their attention away from the woman's transgressions to their own sinfulness.

If we use this Lent for the same purpose, to turn our attention to our own sinfulness, we might start by considering when and why we've acted like the scribes and Pharisees— holding up someone else's shortcomings to serve our purposes. Although we feign dismay at the fact that a relative or friend no longer attends Mass or perhaps has left the Church altogether, do we secretly derive satisfaction from the fact that time has proven us to be the "better Catholic"? When someone else's child gets into trouble, are we quick to point out the deficiencies in the way he was raised so as to implicitly demonstrate the superiority of our own approach? When a co-worker is let go, is there a part of us that revels in the idea that we made the cut while the other person did not, and takes it as an assurance of our competence?

The Evangelist tells us that when Jesus invited the one without sin to cast the first stone, "They went away, one by one, beginning with the elders." (John 8:9) During these 40 days, may our awareness of our own sinfulness lead us, like the chastened scribes and Pharisees, away from condemnation of others.

For Reflection:

1. What actions or wrong-doing by others in my own life (not in the news) most angers me? What does the fact that these particular actions upset me so greatly tell me about myself?

2. When did I last condemn or criticize someone else? What were my motives—*all* of my motives, including the ones I don't acknowledge to others and maybe don't even like to acknowledge to myself? What did I have to gain in terms of public perception, self-image, or other benefit from my condemnation or criticism?

3. When someone in my life falls short or is "caught in the act," how can I stay mindful of my own sinfulness and of Christ's command to show mercy so as to resist becoming part of the crowd that gathers in condemnation? How can I instead reach out to a fellow sinner in humility and without judgment?

FRIDAY, SECOND WEEK OF LENT
THE WOMAN CAUGHT IN ADULTERY

"Early in the morning he came again to the temple. All the people came to him and he sat down and began to teach them. The scribes and the Pharisees brought a woman who had been caught in adultery; and making her stand before all of them, they said to him, 'Teacher, this woman was caught in the very act of committing adultery. Now in the law Moses commanded us to stone such women. Now what do you say?' They said this to test him, so that they might have some charge to bring against him. Jesus bent down and wrote with his finger on the ground. When they kept on questioning him, he straightened up and said to them, 'Let anyone among you who is without sin be the first to throw a stone at her.' And once again he bent down and wrote on the ground. When they heard it, they went away, one by one, beginning with the elders; and Jesus was left alone with the woman standing before him. Jesus straightened up and said to her, 'Woman, where are they? Has no one condemned you?' She said, 'No one, sir.' And Jesus said, 'Neither do I condemn you. Go your way, and from now on do not sin again.'"

John 8:2-11

We live in a society in which movie actors whose careers are faltering seek to stay in the public eye by making sex tapes that "somehow get leaked" and end up on the Internet. In an environment where almost all things sexual are accepted and even celebrated, it is impossible for us to appreciate the humiliation, much less the abject fear, which the woman in this Gospel passage must have experienced.

Sure, we all have at least a couple of embarrassing episodes seared into our memory, and can readily recall an occasion when we were chastised publicly for doing something wrong. But I strongly suspect—and certainly hope—that none

89

of us has been through anything that even remotely compares with this woman's ordeal. To be "caught in the very act" during one of life's most intimate moments is traumatizing enough for anyone at any time, but adultery in the era of Jesus carried a crushing sense of shame that has been greatly diluted in our age of "sexual liberation." And beyond the humiliation and shame lay death—imminent and horrible –as the crowd of men swarming around and ogling and scolding this unfortunate woman soon enough would turn their gazes from leering at her to appraising the size and heft of nearby stones.

A few times a year we read news accounts of stonings or other ghastly punishments in regions where the harshest interpretation of Islamic law still is applied. We recoil from the brutality (as does the overwhelming majority of the world's Muslims), and a public outcry invariably results. It's terrible, but it is so alien to our lives, so far removed from our experience, that beyond shuddering at the idea, we don't give it much thought.

The woman in the Gospel didn't have that luxury. For her, there was nothing remote about the idea of death by stoning. As far as she knew, it could well be her fate—one that she would meet in just a few minutes.

And yet, for all that separates us from this woman as measured by years and settings and societal attitudes, we have more in common with her than we might at first realize.

First, she is our sister in sin. We may not (or may) have committed the same sin as she did, but we have committed and will commit plenty of other sins in our own right. Second, we, too, have been "caught in the very act." The God who sees all and knows all has seen and knows all the wrong we've done. (Of course, He also knows all the good we've done, including that not recognized or appreciated by others.)

But the most important thing we have in common with this woman is found in the dynamic of her encounter with Jesus. The Evangelist tells us that after Jesus had caused the scribes and Pharisees to recognize their own sinfulness, prompting them to drift away, Jesus "was left alone with the woman standing before him." (John 8:9) There will come a day when we, too, find ourselves standing alone before Jesus. We will be in the same state as the adulterous woman, with nothing to cover our faults, with our sin absolutely apparent. Like her, we will be facing judgment, but this time it won't be our mortal life that is at stake; it will be our eternal fate.

That's a sobering prospect, one that rightly worries us. But lest we become discouraged, remember who it is that we will be standing before, and what He had done for this woman just prior to their one-on-one encounter. He had saved her life. He had used his power to help her avoid what was, by the standards of her society, her just sentence. And that is exactly what Jesus already has done for us. Through His passion, death, and resurrection, He has used His power to help us avoid the consequences of our sin. That's what He and His Father want for us, if we will but accept it. As Jesus says later in the Gospel, "I came not to judge the world, but to save the world." (John 12:47)

Those words offer us tremendous re-assurance. However, if we are to receive the eternal gift that they portend, we need to hear and understand them in their full context, and respond accordingly. Jesus spoke at a point between His triumphal entry into Jerusalem and the beginning of His Passion. John tells us that Jesus "cried aloud" in frustration, because so many people who had heard His teachings refused to believe due to fear or spiritual blindness or hard-heartedness. And so what Jesus had to say was equal parts warning and promise:

> "Whoever believes in me believes not in me but in him who sent me. And whoever sees me sees him who sent me. I have come as light into the world, so that everyone who believes in me should not remain in the darkness. I do not judge anyone who hears my words and does not keep them, for I came not to judge the world, but to save the world. The one who rejects me and does not receive my word has a judge; on the last day the word that I have spoken will serve as judge, for I have not spoken on my own, but the Father who sent me has himself given me a commandment about what to say and what to speak. And I know that his commandment is eternal life. What I speak, therefore, I speak just as the Father has told me." (John 12:44-50)

We can't know whether it will occur this week, this month, this year, or not for many, many years, but we do know that, like the woman in the Gospel, we will find ourselves standing alone before Jesus one day. Let us use this Lent to prepare ourselves, by hearing, accepting, and observing His words, so that on the last day, there will be no cause to condemn us.

For Reflection:

1. Which sins cause me the most shame, and will be the most painful to acknowledge before the Lord? What can I change in my life to avoid the circumstances that lead me to commit these sins?

2. When was the last time I availed myself of the sacrament of reconciliation? When can I go next, and how can I engage in a thorough examination of conscience beforehand so as to make a good confession? Do I accept—truly accept—the forgiveness bestowed by God through my confessor? If not, why not, and how can I develop greater faith in the reality that God's love and power to forgive are infinitely greater than my failings and power to do wrong?

3. How can I balance acknowledgment of my sinfulness and shortcomings with a healthy realization of the good things that I do and my intrinsic worth and dignity as a beloved child of God?

4. What can I do this Lent—and going forward—to truly hear, accept, and observe the word of God?

SATURDAY, SECOND WEEK OF LENT
THE BELIEVERS TO WHOM JESUS OFFERED
THE TRUTH

"Then Jesus said to the Jews who had believed in him, 'If you continue in my word, you are truly my disciples; and you will know the truth, and the truth will make you free.' They answered him, 'We are descendants of Abraham and have never been slaves to anyone. What do you mean by saying, 'You will be made free'?' Jesus answered them, 'Very truly, I tell you, everyone who commits sin is a slave to sin.'"
John 8:31-34

Thanks, but no thanks.

That, in essence, was the answer that many of those who had come to believe in Jesus gave the Lord when He offered them the knowledge of the truth and the freedom that derive from remaining in His word and thus being His disciples.

We modern-day believers in Jesus often have the same response to God's invitation.

Sometimes, we just don't want to be free. Not if the prerequisite is knowing the truth about ourselves. That old saying, "The truth hurts" is very—well—true, and sometimes we would rather not face unpleasant realities, even if the price of our denial is continued subjection to people and things and forces that we have allowed to acquire power over us. It is for this reason that many experts in addiction medicine say that you can't begin to help someone with a drinking or drug problem until they acknowledge that they *have* a drinking or drug problem.

Or perhaps we reject freedom because we can't envision being without the things or feelings that have usurped our liberty. We all know that many alcoholics won't stop drinking because they fear the pain of facing life sober. But is it possible that we're afraid to break free of the materialism that not only feeds our desire for things but that also validates our self-worth by allowing us to point to the size of our salary or home as proof of our value? Do we even acknowledge the extent to which we've been influenced by our consumerist society, or do we justify our acquisitive mindset with the excuse that, "We're only working to provide a good life for our children" or, "There's nothing wrong with enjoying the results of my hard work"? And, of course, there *is* nothing wrong with providing for your family and benefitting from your talents and efforts—so long as those wholesome attitudes and activities don't mask a darker reality of thinking that your intrinsic value owes not to your status as a child of God but rather depends on your material success.

A half century before the birth of Christ, the Roman historian Sallust wrote, "Few men desire freedom; the majority seek nothing more than fair masters." The problem is that there is only one truly fair master, the one who offers us not only truth and freedom but also eternal life. The more we subject ourselves to other masters, the more we realize how unfair they are. We give up our freedom only to find that our new "master" isn't keeping its end of the bargain, and instead demands ever more of us for ever less in return. That was a lesson learned in the last century by people seduced into surrendering their liberty by the false promises of Fascism, Nazism, and Communism.

Thank goodness we in the United States aren't subject to the same danger. Just as the people to whom Jesus spoke dismissed His offer by saying, "We are descendants of Abraham and have never been slaves to anyone" (John 8:33), we reject any suggestion of our dependence by saying, "We are Americans. We are a free people in a free country, and have never been enslaved to anything." So disregard what our credit card debts, and our obesity, and our patronage of plastic surgeons and "gentlemen's clubs" might indicate about the things to which we are beholden.

But if we have the courage to ask ourselves whether, in all honesty, we are free, Christ tells us how to find the answer. "If you continue in my word, you are truly my disciples, and you will know the truth, and the truth will make you free." (John 8:31-32)

So the key to discipleship, and to finding the truth, and ultimately to being free, is to "continue in my word." And this is the paradox that so many people cannot accept.

These are the people (perhaps including ourselves at certain times) who bristle at the notion of the "Church telling us what to do." They criticize the Church for laying too many obligations and guilt trips and "thou shalt nots" on us, and for trying to extend its writ into even the most intimate aspects of our lives.

What business does the Church have to seek such power over us? Disregard, for a moment, the fact that it is the institution created by Christ to continue His mission on earth and that it has been guided by the Holy Spirit, as Jesus promised it would, since Pentecost. Set aside, as well, the fact that it explicitly affirms the role of conscience in the individual Christian's response to its teachings. But acknowledge, at the least, that in surviving and thriving for more than 2,000 years despite persecutions, scandals, revolutions, societal upheavals, technological advances, and all the changes and challenges of 20 centuries, the Church has come to know a thing or two about human nature.

It knows, for instance, that the consequences of "sexual freedom" can be measured not only in cases of venereal disease and numbers of abortions but also in the emotional callousness that comes from defining sexuality downward to sex devoid of commitment and in the diminution of intimacy between a husband and wife when each comes to their marriage with a history of numerous sexual partners. It knows that all of the earthly things that promise to fulfill our desires soon enough leave us feeling empty and chasing the even-bigger house, even-better high, even-greater honor until our lives become one long fool's errand. And it knows that the way to be free from the fear, heartache, and perpetual dissatisfaction that come from exercising our freedom to pursue that which would enslave us is to surrender our lives to the God who surrendered His for us.

This Lent, may we strive to continue in the word of God, so that we will have the insight and courage to see and accept those truths about ourselves that will make us truly free.

For Reflection:

1. What truths about myself, and about the extent to which I have become unhealthily beholden to people, things, behaviors, or feelings, am I reluctant to acknowledge? What hurts do such truths cause, and why? How can I bring this truth to God, secure in the knowledge that He already is aware of it and waits with His understanding and love to heal the hurt that this truth causes me?

2. To what have I surrendered my freedom? How and why did this happen? Has the reward proven worth the cost? How can I reclaim my freedom by "continuing in the word" of God?

3. What teachings or requirements of the Church do I find most difficult to obey, or have I perhaps chosen not to follow? Have I shared my difficulties and questions and disagreements with a priest? What would happen if I experimented with "radical trust" and, at least for a set period, followed the teaching or requirement despite not understanding or agreeing with it?

MONDAY, THIRD WEEK OF LENT
THE MAN BORN BLIND

"As he walked along, he saw a man blind from birth. His disciples asked him, 'Rabbi, who sinned, this man or his parents, that he was born blind?' Jesus answered, 'Neither this man nor his parents sinned; he was born blind so that God's works might be revealed in him. We must work the works of him who sent me while it is day; night is coming when no one can work. As long as I am in the world, I am the light of the world.' When he had said this, he spat on the ground and made mud with the saliva and spread the mud on the man's eyes, saying to him, 'Go, wash in the pool of Siloam' (which means Sent). Then he went and washed and came back able to see. The neighbors and those who had seen him before as a beggar began to ask, 'Is this not the man who used to sit and beg?' Some were saying, 'It is he.' Others were saying, 'No, but it is someone like him.' He kept saying, 'I am the man.' But they kept asking him, 'Then how were your eyes opened?' He answered, 'The man called Jesus made mud, spread it on my eyes, and said to me, 'Go to Siloam and wash.' Then I went and washed and received my sight.' They said to him, 'Where is he?' He said, 'I do not know.'

They brought to the Pharisees the man who had formerly been blind. Now it was a sabbath day when Jesus made the mud and opened his eyes. Then the Pharisees also began to ask him how he had received his sight. He said to them, 'He put mud on my eyes. Then I washed, and now I see.' Some of the Pharisees said, 'This man is not from God, for he does not observe the sabbath.' But others said, 'How can a man who is a sinner perform such signs?' And they were divided. So they said again to the blind man, 'What do you say about him? It was your eyes he opened.' He said, 'He is a prophet.'"

John 9:1-17

This story of blindness and vision is, fittingly enough, rich in insights, particularly into the difference between how God sees and how we often look at things. The passage opens with the disciples encountering a blind man and immediately wanting to assign blame. Who is at fault, they want to know, the man or his parents?

How often do we do the same? We hear that friends are divorcing, and our first step isn't to reach out to support them or their children but to dissect their marriage and debate which spouse shoulders the majority of the blame for the break-up. We learn that the neighbors' son has gotten into trouble with the law or is failing in school, and our initial reaction isn't to lend a helping hand but to consider all the ways their child-rearing was inferior to ours. We see a poor person and automatically attribute his plight to laziness, lack of intelligence, or perhaps drug use.

Contrast that approach with how Jesus saw matters and answered the disciples' question. He dismissed the issues of sin and blame, and went to the heart of the matter: how God uses the infirm as well as the healthy, the weak as well as the strong, to make His glory manifest.

In our day as in Jesus' time, we admire the strong and the powerful. They are the movers and shakers, the people who matter and who get things done. Even more than in Jesus' day, our society values productivity, and has made a cult out of hours logged, sales tallied, and compensation earned (and then spent extravagantly).

In enlisting a blind beggar to serve his purpose, Jesus rejects all of this. So, too, does His Church today in raising a prophetic voice against the dangers of equating a human being's intrinsic worth and dignity with his or her productivity. Make no

102

mistake; that is the dark corollary to an unhealthy regard for productivity and achievement. When we go beyond an appropriate respect for achievement to the equivalent of hero worship, we inevitably embrace the accompanying notion that those who have achieved little as measured in material terms are somehow unworthy and not entitled to the respect owed to every person solely by virtue of being a son or daughter of God.

These false distinctions are used to justify the continued marginalization of minorities whose progress had been blocked in years past by institutional barriers and continues to be constrained by enduring prejudice, and to rationalize policies that begrudge poor people the assistance they need to improve their lives. This specious linkage between a person's productivity and intrinsic value also provides a philosophical and visceral rationale for abortion, euthanasia, and for relegating to second-class status the physically and mentally disabled, the aged, and the infirm.

Now let's consider how Jesus gave this man his sight. The Lord directed the beggar to go to the Pool of Siloam and, once there, to wash the clay, or dirt, from his eyes. The Gospel tells us that Siloam means "sent," a fitting translation given that Jesus directed, or sent, the beggar to a place where he would obtain the gift of sight. We need the faith to believe that God will guide each of us to the place where we can see things as they truly are—if we will allow Him to direct us as the blind beggar did.

Similarly, in order to see with the eyes of faith, we need to wash away the dirt that can cloud our vision. When we fall into patterns of sin, our perceptions become warped. Against these impediments to clear vision, the Church offers the spiritual equivalent of Lasik surgery in the Sacrament of Reconciliation.

This incredibly liberating, tragically under-utilized, sacrament brings the penitent to the place where he or she can wash away the dirt clouding his vision by confessing his transgressions to the priest. I can't help but think that those who argue that there's no need to verbalize one's sins to another human being when you can "go directly to God" have not experienced the profound sense of relief that comes from "owning" one's faults aloud and then receiving the assurance of the priest, acting with the authority bestowed by Jesus himself ("If you forgive the sins of any, they are forgiven them; if you retain the sins of any, they are retained" John 20:23), that you have been absolved and forgiven by the power of the Holy Spirit.

Finally, let's consider the varied reactions to the blind man gaining his sight. His neighbors responded to this amazing development not with rejoicing, but with consternation and suspicion. Some even refused to believe he was the same man they had long known. They marched him off to the Pharisees, who showed their profound near-sightedness by focusing exclusively on the fact that Jesus performed this miracle on the Sabbath in an apparent violation of Jewish law. Like us, they saw what they wanted to see, and had no trouble ignoring the bigger picture in order to find something they could criticize in someone they disliked.

Then there is the blind man himself. His gift of sight was so new to him that he had not yet become adept at shading and screening and squinting and all the other visual tricks we regularly employ so that things appear the way we think they should. The neighbors and Pharisees asked him what happened, and he answered with the simple, unvarnished truth: "The man called Jesus made clay and anointed my eyes and told me, 'Go to Siloam and wash.' Then I went and washed and received my sight." When they then asked him what he had to say about

Jesus, he gave the only rational answer anyone could, given what he had just experienced: "He is a prophet." May our spiritual efforts this Lent give us the same clarity to see things as they actually are and the same courage to speak the simple truth about what it is we see.

For Reflection:

1. Thinking back to when I last heard bad news about someone, what was my first, instinctive reaction? What does that reaction say about me and my attitudes? How can I become a more-compassionate and less-judgmental person? Who in my life can I reach out to today or this week to provide genuine support in a time of trouble or need, and what can I do for them that will be truly meaningful?

2. How can I act in defense of those in our society who are marginalized because they lack power or strength, or do not meet societal norms for being sufficiently productive? What can I do in the days ahead for a specific individual that will affirm his or her intrinsic worth and dignity?

3. What shortcomings or patterns of sin may be distorting my ability to see things as they truly are? How am I "kidding myself" or rationalizing things to avoid facing unpleasant truths about myself? When was the last time I made use of the Sacrament of Reconciliation, and when will I go again?

4. What simple truth am I perhaps not stating because it does not accord with the prevailing view, and how can I best express it?

TUESDAY, THIRD WEEK OF LENT
THE BLIND MAN'S PARENTS

"The Jews did not believe that he had been blind and had received his sight
until they called the parents of the man who had received his sight and
asked them, 'Is this your son, who you say was born blind? How then does
he now see?' His parents answered, 'We know that this is our son, and
that he was born blind; but we do not know how it is that now he sees, nor
do we know who opened his eyes. Ask him; he is of age. He will speak for
himself.' His parents said this because they were afraid of the Jews; for the
Jews had already agreed that anyone who confessed Jesus to be the Messiah
would be put out of the synagogue. Therefore his parents said,
'He is of age; ask him.'"
John 9:18-23

Half truths and long distances.

How many families today operate with the formula
employed by the blind man's parents?

Faced with expulsion from the synagogue if they told all
that they knew about their son and his healing by Jesus, the blind
man's parents opted to acknowledge only half the truth—the
safe half. Yes, he is our child, and yes, he was born blind. As to
how he suddenly is able to see, don't ask us; ask him. What the
parents' answer lacked in candor it made up for in distance. They
were trying to place themselves as far as possible from their son's
situation to avoid the societal consequences.

How often in our own family relationships do we
choose to acknowledge "the safe half" of the truth? We take

pride, rightly, in our devotion to our children and all that we do to meet their needs and put them on track for a bright future. But we don't acknowledge that some of that effort comes at the expense of attention to our husband or wife, in part because there are times when it's just easier and more gratifying to be a parent than a spouse. We remain estranged from a sibling years after a fight, remembering, accurately, all the spiteful things he said during that terrible confrontation. But we're slow to recognize that we said some pretty awful things, too, and that we took cheap shots aimed squarely at vulnerabilities that only a brother or sister would know.

At other times, recognizing only "the safe half" of the truth isn't a matter of ignoring our own faults and failings but rather of denying realities that are at odds with our vision of how we want our families to be. Attributing a daughter's lackluster academic performance to the fact that "she just isn't a good test-taker," is easier than acknowledging that while the young woman can be successful in any number of fields, she lacks the work ethic and intellectual gifts needed to fulfill *your* dream that she become a physician, or attorney, or astrophysicist. Reveling in the fact that everyone sees your husband as "the life of the party" is far more enticing than owning up to the reality that he is drinking too much too often.

A second option when family members don't meet our expectations or figure prominently in our plans or priorities is to put distance between them and us. Sometimes that distance is a literal one, measurable in hundreds or even thousands of miles. More often, however, it is emotional distance—words that remain unspoken, time that is allowed to go by, conscious and subconscious decisions to cause or allow separation. Like the blind man's parents, our decision to distance ourselves from family members can be driven by the desire to avoid societal consequences. You know that you should invite your husband's sister to that big surprise birthday party that you're planning for him but, frankly, she chose a very different path in life and would have nothing in common with the friends from your more-affluent town who are so dear to you. Why invite her to an event where she would just feel awkward and out of place? It's her feelings that you're thinking about. Besides, you'll be plenty busy that night; you won't have time to take her around and make all the introductions, much less keep an eye out to ensure that she's not saying something embarrassing to one of your friends.

At other times, the decision to place societal standing over family is not even recognized for what it is. We know we should visit our elderly parents more often, we really do, but with a son in both a town and a travel soccer league and a daughter signed up for jazz and hip-hop and ballet dance classes (and don't forget her voice lessons), our weekends just aren't our own. In a society where middle-aged adults often live vicariously through their children, many people aren't willing to suffer the consequences of opting out of overloaded sports and performing-arts schedules to bring balance to their family lives. If volunteering at a senior citizen center will help burnish a high school junior's college application, we'll make time for that, but the same time isn't available for the young man or woman to spend a Sunday afternoon with his or her grandparents.

There is, of course, a third option. It involves setting aside our pride and our fear, that which we desire and that which we dread, to see ourselves and our families as we truly are. It requires "closing the gap" between our idealized vision and our reality, and between ourselves and those members of our family who don't always meet our expectations and with whom we don't always get along. It can be a painful process, because it requires surrendering much in order to gain much, and because it will work only if we can exercise, or at least try to exercise, unconditional love. Although we're loathe to admit it, unconditional love is at odds with the way our society operates and the way we've been taught to think. Society functions on the basis of the quid pro quo. I work this many hours for you, and in return you pay me this much money. I give you this much money, and in return you sell me these many groceries. While this is an entirely rational way to conduct our business affairs, it fails miserably within the context of a family. When it comes to how we treat our relatives and, ultimately, all people, only the radical love preached by Jesus—giving without seeking gain and sowing without regard to reaping—will do. It is incredibly hard to practice this kind of love, but if we allow Jesus to open our eyes as He did those of the blind man, we will have the vision we need to close the distances that too long have separated us from one another.

For Reflection:

1. What half truths color my perception of my family and of me? How can I turn to the one who is "the way, the truth, and the life" for help in acknowledging the full truth and acting in a way that reflects that reality?

2. What separations have I initiated or allowed to occur with other members of my family? Why did I do that? How can I begin to "close the gap" in a way that is healthy for me and respectful of my relative(s)?

3. Are there times when I have allowed societal expectations or pressures to create distance between me and someone in my family? What were the circumstances, and how can I rectify the situation?

4. What can I do today, or this week, for a relative that involves giving without seeking any type of return or gain—material, emotional, or otherwise?

Wednesday, Third Week of Lent
The Blind Man's Interrogators

"So for the second time they called the man who had been blind, and they said to him, 'Give glory to God! We know that this man is a sinner.' He answered, 'I do not know whether he is a sinner. One thing I do know, that though I was blind, now I see.' They said to him, 'What did he do to you? How did he open your eyes?' He answered them, 'I have told you already, and you would not listen. Why do you want to hear it again? Do you also want to become his disciples?' Then they reviled him, saying, 'You are his disciple, but we are disciples of Moses. We know that God has spoken to Moses, but as for this man, we do not know where he comes from.' The man answered, 'Here is an astonishing thing! You do not know where he comes from, and yet he opened my eyes. We know that God does not listen to sinners, but he does listen to one who worships him and obeys his will. Never since the world began has it been heard that anyone opened the eyes of a person born blind. If this man were not from God, he could do nothing.' They answered him, 'You were born entirely in sins, and are you trying to teach us?' And they drove him out.

Jesus heard that they had driven him out, and when he found him, he said, 'Do you believe in the Son of Man?' He answered, 'And who is he, sir? Tell me, so that I may believe in him.' Jesus said to him, 'You have seen him, and the one speaking with you is he.' He said, 'Lord, I believe.' And he worshiped him. Jesus said, 'I came into this world for judgment so that those who do not see may see, and those who do see may become blind.'"

John 9:24-39

Seeing isn't always believing.

Not when what our eyes take in is dissonant with our experience and expectations. And that's not necessarily a bad thing. Get a few years under your belt, and you learn the truth in the saying,

"Appearances can be deceiving." From three-card monte hucksters ensnaring gullible tourists on city streets to smooth "investment counselors," charismatic politicians, and home-repair scam artists, we know that people can present alluring images that hide ugly realities, or that distract our gaze while just beyond our peripheral vision a confederate is, as the phrase so aptly puts it, "robbing us blind."

So, being wise to the ways of the world, we're a sensible, skeptical people, and we carry those attitudes into our faith life. Rather than be lured away from the Church and its teachings by the latest New Age fad, glib televangelist or theological innovation, we trust the magisterium. For its part, the Church guards the faith and the faithful by bringing a high degree of caution and rigor to responding to everything from reports of miracles, apparitions, and possessions to calls for the canonization of those who seemingly led lives of heroic Christian virtue.

The challenge is ensuring that a proper concern for orthodoxy and a determination to not be misled don't devolve into a blindness or deafness that make us miss a perfectly sound message because of our preconceived notions about the messenger.

The Pharisees weren't open to hearing anything good about Jesus from *anyone*. But it must have been particularly galling to hear testimony in support of this ersatz rabbi from a man who had been born blind. In their society, physical disability was considered a divine punishment for sin, committed either by the afflicted person or his parents. The Pharisees, by comparison, scrupulously followed every rule and commandment in order to be pleasing to God—and well-pleased with themselves. So the thought that this manifest sinner would have something to tell them about faith and God was not only ludicrous, it was downright offensive.

But the man could see. That was the problem. They knew he had been blind from birth, and there was no denying that now he had his vision. Others knew that, as well, and were beginning to believe in Jesus as a result. This couldn't be. So, because the Pharisees couldn't accept what they saw, they chose to see what they could accept. In rejecting the reality that a man born blind now could see, those who had been born with sight made themselves blind to the truth. Just as Jesus said would be the response to His mission and message. (John 9:39)

Our biases can distort our perceptions, too, both in terms of what we see firsthand and in the way we "edit" what we see or hear to conform to our expectations before relaying it to others. In the late 1940s, psychologists Gordon W. Allport and Leo Postman conducted an experiment in which they showed people an illustration of a white man in casual clothes holding a razor and confronting a black man wearing a suit and tie on a subway car. The "eyewitnesses" then related what they had seen to others, who in turn described the scene to a third set of participants, and so on. In keeping with the prevailing prejudices of their (and our) time, the story hadn't gone through many rounds of re-telling before many of the white participants had "transferred" the razor into the hand of the African-American, occasionally adding lurid tidbits about the black man waving the weapon around wildly. Was this inaccuracy attributable to nothing more sinister than a manifestation of the "Telephone Game" phenomenon, in which more and more details of an original message are dropped or distorted with each successive telling? Extremely unlikely; none of the African-American participants made the mistake of shifting the razor from the one man to the other when they described the scene.* If we don't guard against such prejudices we can easily miss the word of God spoken to us by unlikely sources.

We'll dismiss the woman who spent her early adult years in a Bohemian lifestyle, living with a number of men in succession and even having an abortion. Like Dorothy Day.

We'll ignore the unskilled laborer whose alcoholism at one point dragged him to such depths that he would steal to come up with the money he needed to drink. Like Venerable Matthew Talbot.

We'll reject the men and women who foolishly rejected wealth and comfort and prominence for a life of evangelical poverty. Like Francis and Clare and so many other saints down through the ages.

We'll rebuff those who come from places we've never heard of and speak with accents we sometimes can't understand. Like all the wonderful priests from Africa and Asia who have traveled far from their homes to serve the People of God in the United States and to help re-evangelize our country.

On a more basic level, we'll not hear the neighbor or co-worker or friend whose words of support or challenge, whose question or advice, can lead us to a closer relationship with God.

We need to be thoughtful and prudent. We need to consider if what we're seeing or being told accords with the teachings of the Church. We need to remember Christ's own

---

* Allport GW, and Postman LJ. 1947. <u>The Psychology of Rumor</u>. New York: Russell & Russell

guidance regarding those who would lead us this way or that: "You will know them by their fruits." (Matthew 7:16) But we also need to be open, and to recognize that the Lord can select the most unlikely messengers to speak on His behalf.

With his new vision, the man born blind was able to recognize the Lord. This Lent, let us ask Him who promises, "See, I am making all things new" (Revelation 21:5) to give our world-weary eyes the ability to see with a new faith the hand of God at work in those around us.

For Reflection:

1. Are there specific individuals or types of people I don't hear because I think I'm a "better Catholic" than they are or in some other way am superior to them? How can I rid myself of that attitude, show them the respect of listening attentively to what they have to say, and then consider carefully whether, in matters of faith or other areas, I can learn something from them?

2. This Lent, how can I cultivate the faith and vision needed to heed St. Ignatius of Loyola's urging to "see God in all things?"

3. What are the blind spots in my faith life? Are there any realities I don't see or won't see because they would require me to change or grow in ways I don't want? How can I increase my trust that the Lord will give me not only the vision but also the strength and direction I need to draw closer to Him?

Thursday, Third Week of Lent
Martha

"When Jesus arrived, he found that Lazarus had already been in the tomb four days. Now Bethany was near Jerusalem, some two miles away, and many of the Jews had come to Martha and Mary to console them about their brother. When Martha heard that Jesus was coming, she went and met him, while Mary stayed at home. Martha said to Jesus, 'Lord, if you had been here, my brother would not have died. But even now I know that God will give you whatever you ask of him.' Jesus said to her, 'Your brother will rise again.' Martha said to him, 'I know that he will rise again in the resurrection on the last day.' Jesus said to her, 'I am the resurrection and the life. Those who believe in me, even though they die, will live, and everyone who lives and believes in me will never die. Do you believe this?' She said to him, 'Yes, Lord, I believe that you are the Messiah, the Son of God, the one coming into the world.'"

John 11:17-27

Jesus certainly didn't have our sense of timing.

When we want to ask someone to put their faith in us, we wait for the ideal moment.

We wait until we've completed a major project or closed a big deal to ask for a raise or promotion. We wait for Christmas or New Year's Eve or Valentine's Day to propose, making sure that we've arranged every detail to create just the right atmosphere before popping the question. In short, we don't ask an important question until we've done all we can to ensure that the timing is right and that we'll receive the answer we want.

Not Jesus. He probably couldn't have picked a worse time to ask Martha for her declaration of faith. Her brother had died just a few days before. What was worse, she and her sister had sent for Jesus when Lazarus fell ill, and after receiving the news he delayed for two days before setting out for Bethany.

And yet, when Martha learns that Jesus finally is approaching and goes out to meet him, there's no hint of reproach in her statement, "Lord, if you had been here, my brother would not have died." The words are a statement of faith, not an accusation. She didn't say, "Where were you? Why didn't you come as soon as we sent for you? This is all your fault." Instead, she stated the fact of the matter as she firmly believed it to be.

And that graciousness and confidence in Jesus in the face of tragedy wasn't enough for the Lord. He wanted more. When Jesus told her that Lazarus would rise and she, thinking He was referring to the resurrection on the last day, affirmed her belief in eternal life, that wasn't enough for Jesus. He wanted to still more.

So Jesus put the question to her point blank: "I am the resurrection and the life. Those who believe in me, even though they die, will live, and everyone who lives and believes in me will never die. Do you believe this?" (John 11:25-26)

It was a question that demanded a Yes or a No. There was no room for hedging, or for talking in generalities about our essence somehow going on after death, and how if people lead a good life overall surely there has to be something more for them than this, and all the other rambling responses we use to dance around the cosmic question of our everlasting fate. Jesus said, in essence, Fine, you believe in eternal life. What I want to know is whether you believe that *I am* the resurrection and the life, the way to Heaven?

Jesus asks the same question of each of us and, often—as was the case with Martha—at the worst possible times.

We have no trouble asserting our faith in good times. When we're standing godparent for an infant, and the priest or deacon asks us to make the baptismal vows on the child's behalf, we readily attest to the precepts of the faith that are read aloud to us. We're happy to do the same when the congregation renews the baptismal vows at Mass during the Easter season. We answer reflexively, being honest, but not really thinking that much about what we're saying.

An honest answer is much more difficult to provide, and is hardly offered reflexively, when we are asked the question at other times in our life, times when the answer really, really matters. After someone we love has been taken from us—or has chosen to leave us. After the job that provided not only our financial security but also our sense of self-worth comes to an end. After the doctor has confirmed what we suspected, and dreaded, all along.

That's when we are Martha.

And, like Martha, we have choices to make. As the Evangelist tells us, after Lazarus had been in the tomb for four days, ". . . many of the Jews had come to Martha and Mary to console them about their brother. When Martha heard that Jesus was coming, she went and met him, while Mary stayed at home." (John 11:19-20)

When bad news arrives, when our earthly hopes and desires have been buried, friends are of great comfort, but it is

121

only the Lord who brings true hope and healing, and we must encounter Him alone. While Mary remained at home surrounded by friends and neighbors, Martha went out, by herself, to find the Lord.

Once we encounter Jesus, we need to make our second choice. Will we chide Him and blame Him for our troubles, perhaps even rejecting Him in the belief that He has rejected us? Will we try to bargain and deal with Him, seeking to extract a miracle as the price of our assent? Or will we, like Martha, express our faith in God and our confidence that the end of our earthly dreams, and even our earthly life, is not the end of us?

And, finally, we have to answer the same question that Jesus put to Martha. Not whether we believe in some generalized "higher power" or "deity" or "collective consciousness." And not whether we believe that we live on in the memory of those who loved us or that our spirit is immutable or that "a better place" awaits. We need to tell Jesus whether we believe He is all that He told us He is: the resurrection and the life; the way, the truth, and the life; the Messiah; the Son of God; the savior of the world. It isn't an essay question, or an SAT question allowing the student to choose from among four answers. Our only options are Yes and No.

May God give us the grace this Lent to strengthen our faith, so that each time we are asked that question, on occasions of joy and on occasions of great trial and sorrow, we can respond without hesitation in the words of Martha, "Yes, Lord."

For Reflection:

1. On what occasions have I hedged or wavered in acknowledging Jesus as the resurrection and the life? What drove my doubts at that time, and how can I increase my faith now, so that it will be strong when my beliefs are put to the test?

2. How can I increase the time I spend alone with Jesus now—such as in prayer and at Eucharistic Adoration—in preparation for the day when I will meet Him alone at the end of my life?

3. What are some other ways I can say "Yes" to God now, in other matters of faith and Christian service, so that I will be better able to offer an unhesitating, heart-felt "Yes" to the question of accepting Him as the resurrection and the life, my Lord and Savior?

FRIDAY, THIRD WEEK OF LENT
LAZARUS

"When Mary came where Jesus was and saw him, she knelt at his feet and said to him, 'Lord, if you had been here, my brother would not have died.' When Jesus saw her weeping, and the Jews who came with her also weeping, he was greatly disturbed in spirit and deeply moved. He said, 'Where have you laid him?' They said to him, 'Lord, come and see.' Jesus began to weep. So the Jews said, 'See how he loved him!' But some of them said, 'Could not he who opened the eyes of the blind man have kept this man from dying?'

Then Jesus, again greatly disturbed, came to the tomb. It was a cave, and a stone was lying against it. Jesus said, 'Take away the stone.' Martha, the sister of the dead man, said to him, 'Lord, already there is a stench because he has been dead four days.' Jesus said to her, 'Did I not tell you that if you believed, you would see the glory of God?' So they took away the stone. And Jesus looked upward and said, 'Father, I thank you for having heard me. I knew that you always hear me, but I have said this for the sake of the crowd standing here, so that they may believe that you sent me.' When he had said this, he cried with a loud voice, 'Lazarus, come out!' The dead man came out, his hands and feet bound with strips of cloth, and his face wrapped in a cloth. Jesus said to them, 'Unbind him, and let him go.'"

John: 11:32-44

The only thing Lazarus had to do was come out of the cave.

In order to defy death—literally—and to live a new life—again, literally—all Lazarus had to do was heed the voice of Jesus and walk a few short steps toward the Lord. God did everything else.

Because Jesus offers us the same gift of new life that He gave to Lazarus, this Gospel account merits close consideration to better understand how God extends His invitation of eternal life and how we can lay claim to it.

The Lord's sorrow at Martha's distress and Lazarus' situation is a good place to start. The Evangelist tells us that Jesus wept. Our all-powerful and all-knowing God also is an all-caring God. He is with us in our grieving, and doesn't want death, particularly the spiritual death of sin that can separate us from Him forever, to claim any of His children.

God "will go the distance" so that we can avoid that fate. When this chapter of John's Gospel opens, Jesus has just crossed the Jordan to escape the crowds that tried to stone Him and the authorities seeking to arrest Him. He has taken refuge in the wilds where the Baptist had preached. Then word arrives that Lazarus—"he whom you love"—is ill. (John 11:3) The Gospel continues:

> "When Jesus heard it, he said, "This illness does not lead to death; rather it is for God's glory, so that the Son of God may be glorified through it." Accordingly, though Jesus loved Martha and her sister and Lazarus, after having heard that Lazarus was ill, he stayed two days longer in the place where he was. Then after this he said to the disciples, "Let us go to Judea again." The disciples said to him, "Rabbi, the Jews were just now trying to stone you, and are you going there again?" Jesus answered, "Are there not twelve hours of daylight? Those who walk during the day do not stumble, because

they see the light of this world. But those who walk at night stumble, because the light is not in them." (John 11:4-10)

This passage illustrates two things about God's approach that we already know from our own lives but that nonetheless remain difficult to accept.

The first is that God sometimes allows us to experience difficulty and suffer hardship. Jesus could have cured Lazarus the moment He received word of his illness. Instead, He let the illness continue and even progress to death. This wasn't because Jesus was indifferent to Lazarus; Jesus loved him. Rather, the Lord allowed Lazarus' suffering "that the Son of God may be glorified through it," (John 11:4) as occurred when people who witnessed or heard of the raising of Lazarus came to believe in Jesus as a result. When we're sick or in financial difficulties or otherwise facing hardship, the idea that God is using our troubles to His greater glory—often in ways we'll never know— can be cold comfort. Being chosen to assist God in His work in this way is an honor we would just as soon do without. We want a cure or a job or a solution, and we want it now. Which brings us to the second difficult lesson reinforced by this passage: God operates on His timeline, not ours. John writes, "after having heard that Lazarus was ill, he stayed two days longer in the place where he was." (John 11:6) That initial inaction doesn't accord well with our expectations of how someone should respond when a friend is in trouble, or with the pace of our rapid-response culture.

It can be very hard to believe, much less accept, that God is using our difficulties for His greater ends, and that a

127

seeming "delay" in coming to our assistance is not the same as denial of our needs. There's yet another lesson to be gleaned from this passage, however, and hopefully it will enable us to maintain our faith when God doesn't give us the help we want when we want it. That lesson, quite simply, is that Jesus always will come to us; nothing can keep Him away. When Mary and Martha bid Jesus come to their ailing brother, the disciples pleaded with Him not to go, citing the danger involved. Jesus dismissed their concerns out of hand. He was going to Lazarus no matter what.

Again, God will "go the distance for us." Jesus did so by coming to earth and taking on our human form, willingly suffering and dying in reparation for our sins, so that by His passion, death, and resurrection we could have eternal life. The Spirit continues to do so, gently but insistently inviting us to share in the life of grace by turning from sin and embracing God and His commandments.

All we have to do is heed that voice and walk just a few steps toward the Lord. Jesus will command, as He did with Lazarus, that the stones that block our union with Him be moved away. But once they are, we have a choice to make. Will we cower in the darkness, for fear that the stench of our sin is overpowering and that the light outside will be too bright for us to bear? Will we be afraid to move because, like Lazarus, our hands and feet are tied, and our vision obscured? Or will we have the courage and faith to walk toward the voice of Jesus, even though we cannot yet move freely or see clearly?

If, this Lent, we can take just a few halting steps in the direction of the Lord who has journeyed all the way from Heaven to save us, we can be confident that His command to the forces of sin will be the same as He gave the people attending

Lazarus: "Unbind him and let him go." All we have to do is come out of the cave.

For Reflection:

1. Has there been a time in my life when I felt God was indifferent to my difficulties and not hearing or answering my prayers? Looking back on that time, can I now discern ways in which the situation might have proved to be for my ultimate benefit, or that of others?

2. How can I better appreciate that God not only is all-knowing and all-powerful but also all-loving? Can I envision Jesus supporting me when I am discouraged, grieving with and for me in the face of great sorrow, and rejoicing with me in the good things of my life? How, through my prayers, can I bring everything in my life—good and bad—to the Lord?

3. What caves have I fashioned for myself? What makes me fear to leave them, and how can I summon the courage to venture out toward the Lord who waits, just a few steps away, to embrace me?

4. What makes it difficult for me to move toward the Lord? How can I strengthen my faith that God will make my steps, however halting, and my vision, however unclear, sufficient to reach Him if I but make the effort?

SATURDAY, THIRD WEEK OF LENT
MARY AND JUDAS

"Six days before the Passover Jesus came to Bethany, the home of Lazarus, whom he had raised from the dead. There they gave a dinner for him. Martha served, and Lazarus was one of those at the table with him. Mary took a pound of costly perfume made of pure nard, anointed Jesus' feet, and wiped them with her hair. The house was filled with the fragrance of the perfume. But Judas Iscariot, one of his disciples (the one who was about to betray him), said, 'Why was this perfume not sold for three hundred denarii and the money given to the poor?' (He said this not because he cared about the poor, but because he was a thief; he kept the common purse and used to steal what was put into it.) Jesus said, 'Leave her alone. She bought it so that she might keep it for the day of my burial.'"
John: 12:1-7

It's not just what we do; it's why we do it.

The wisdom of the Church's insistence on considering a person's motives as well as his actions is never more evident than in this Gospel passage.

On the surface, Mary would seem to be engaged in extravagant behavior, lavishing a huge amount of expensive oil on Jesus. Thank goodness Judas was there to protest against this indulgence, and to remind everyone how the oil could have been used to raise money for the poor. Except, of course, that his indignation was feigned, and that what he really regretted was not being able to sell the oil for cash that he then could pocket.

131

The Lord knew this—as he knew Mary's genuine devotion and knows all of our true motives—and so rebuked Judas.

We would be wise to remember this story when political parties and interest groups come a-courting.

As Election Day approaches each year, there are those who tell us that, "Catholics can't possibly support the Democratic Party given its position on abortion," while others say with equal vehemence, "There's no way Catholics can vote for Republicans given the impact their economic agenda would have on the poor." No doubt those activists do care about the unborn, or the poor, or the environment, or whatever other cause they invoke, but their primary motive is to win our votes and our money by portraying their party or candidate as in sync with Catholic teaching. They just don't get the truth of what the nation's bishops explained in their 2007 document, *Forming Consciences for Faithful Citizenship*: that the "themes from Catholic social teaching provide a moral framework that does not easily fit ideologies of 'right' or 'left,' 'liberal' or 'conservative,' or the platform of any political party. They are not partisan or sectarian, but reflect fundamental ethical principles that are common to all people."[*]

People who try to assign Catholic teaching a place on the political spectrum are not unlike those who hail Jesus as "a great philosopher" or "the greatest person who ever walked the earth." Those accolades are true, of course, and yet they completely miss the point. If you study the philosophy of Jesus,

---

[*] Section 55, *Forming Consciences for Faithful Citizenship: A Call to Political Responsibility from the Catholic Bishops of the United States*; http://www.usccb.org/issues-and-action/faithful-citizenship/upload/forming-consciences-for-faithful-citizenship.pdf

you will gain rich insights, and if you emulate His conduct, you will lead a moral life. But it's only if you recognize and embrace Him as Son of God, Lord and Savior, that you will secure all that He came to offer us. Similarly, the Gospel and the doctrines of the Church should inform our position on specific issues, but any attempt to reduce them to political manifestos or use them as justification for supporting a particular ideology will fail. They serve a different, higher purpose.

The reality is that all of the political parties—just like all of us—come up short by the standards of the Gospel. That's why the bishops emphasized in *Faithful Citizenship*, "As Catholics, we should be guided more by our moral convictions than by our attachment to a political party or interest group. When necessary, our participation should help transform the party to which we belong; we should not let the party transform us in such a way that we neglect or deny fundamental moral truths."*

If we are guided by our faith, then our positions on issues don't "align with" or "complement" our beliefs as Catholics, they flow directly from those beliefs. The spin doctors and campaign gurus looking for "wedge issues" to "win the Catholic vote" don't understand that premise.

In some instances, of course, the purpose of a "wedge issue" isn't to make inroads with Catholics but rather to drive a wedge between us and the Church. Consider the argument of those who delight in charging, "The Church has too much

---

* Section 14, *Forming Consciences for Faithful Citizenship: A Call to Political Responsibility from the Catholic Bishops of the United States;*
http://www.usccb.org/issues-and-action/faithful-citizenship/upload/forming-consciences-for-faithful-citizenship.pdf

money. It should sell all the artwork in the Vatican and use the money to help the poor."

If all those who are so quick to employ the poor to bash the Church would employ them in actual, paying jobs instead, the poor wouldn't be poor any longer. But, just as in the Gospel passage, that's not really the point or the goal. By remaining in their dire circumstances, the poor serve a useful purpose by providing a cudgel with which to beat up on the clergy, the hierarchy, and the entire Roman Catholic Church for "not doing enough."

Of course, that begs the question of what other institution in the world today and down through the ages operates or has operated more soup kitchens, homeless shelters, orphanages, health clinics, missionary hospitals, low-income housing initiatives, and refugee programs (not to mention hospitals, hospices, grammar schools, high schools, vocational-training programs, and colleges and universities). The assertion also makes no allowance for the hundreds of thousands of religious—starting with Pope Francis I—who lead simple lives in modest settings. But why consider all of the facts when just a few fit your argument so well?

The truth is that it's hard enough to know and acknowledge all of our own motives at times, much less discern those of others. Yet we're called to engage in the great issues of the day, not to sit on the sidelines. So how do we put our faith into action without being used in the process?

Simply follow the example of Mary at the dinner in Bethany: Serve the Lord first and foremost, and tune out the noise generated by those who, like Judas, invoke a deserving cause not out of genuine concern but to advance their own agendas. If our primary aim is to serve God, that desire naturally will lead us to serve His people, and the Spirit—not some campaign strategist or media maven—will direct our efforts to the greatest good.

For Reflection:

1. Can I identify a time when I did the "right" thing for the wrong reason, to serve some hidden agenda of my own? What prompted me to do that, and how can I learn from that incident to avoid repeating that behavior in the future?

2. Similarly, when have I done something for good reasons even though it was not recognized as such, and perhaps even generated criticism? How did I feel in that instance, and how can the knowledge that God knows our true motives strengthen me to persevere in doing the right thing no matter how it is perceived?

3. What aspect of Catholic social teaching really resonates with me, and how can I advocate for a related issue or group of people within our political process in a way that is primarily and authentically Christian?

4. How can I prepare myself through study, prayer, and reflection to defend the Church against unfair or inaccurate criticism in a way that is charitable yet firm and informed?

MONDAY, FOURTH WEEK OF LENT
THE CROWD GREETING JESUS ON HIS ENTRY
TO JERUSALEM

"The next day the great crowd that had come to the festival heard that Jesus was coming to Jerusalem. So they took branches of palm trees and went out to meet him, shouting,

'Hosanna!
Blessed is the one who comes in the name of the Lord—
the King of Israel!'"
John 12:12-13

What percentage, do you think, of the people shouting "Hosanna!" as Jesus entered Jerusalem on Palm Sunday also were among the crowd shouting "Crucify him! Crucify him!" outside Pilate's residence on Good Friday?

If our modern experience in matters far more trivial is any guide, the proportion was fairly high. Witness the excitement when an NFL team signs a new quarterback, and the airwaves are filled with breathless predictions about how he has the potential to transform the franchise into a Superbowl contender (with the player sometimes even being described as the team's "savior"). One loss or a couple of interceptions later, however, and there are cries to "trade the bum" and debate over which college signal-caller entering next year's draft is best matched to the team's offensive style. Politicians and entertainers also are painfully aware of the fickle nature of the periodically adoring

137

public, and work frantically to ride the wave of popularity before it crests and crashes, making way for the next "new sensation."

Consider, then, the welter of emotions the Lord must have felt as He entered Jerusalem. Everyone around Him was ecstatic. The crowds were cheering and putting palm branches and even their cloaks (Mark 11:8) on the road before Him. His disciples, after weeks of laying low for fear of the people and the authorities, had accompanied Jesus to Jerusalem with great trepidation, only to find that their rabbi now was being hailed by the crowds as "the one who comes in the name of the Lord—the King of Israel." (John 12:13) Both onlookers and disciples must have felt that they were present as a great man, perhaps the Messiah, approached His destiny. They were right about that, of course, but only Jesus knew what that destiny was. How sad He must have felt as He looked at the cheering crowds and the shining faces of those jostling to get closer to Him, knowing that within days the crowd would be transformed into a mob howling for His blood, the faces would be contorted into visages of rage, and those closest to Him would be scrambling to get as far away from Him as possible.

In this moment of apparent triumph, the Lord must have known a loneliness and isolation that none of us can even imagine. The loneliness of a sinless man in a sea of sinners. The loneliness of one being cheered by those who soon would execute Him. The loneliness of one surrounded by those He knew would soon would desert Him. The loneliness of God come to earth to pay a terrible price that only He could pay.

Jesus had described the people in that crowd early in His public ministry, in the Parable of the Sower. They were the ones He characterized as the seeds that landed on rocky ground, with insufficient soil to put down lasting roots. The seeds "sprang up quickly, since they had no depth of soil. But when the sun rose, they were scorched; and since they had no root, they withered away." (Matthew 13:5-6)

Like the people who lined the road into Jerusalem on Palm Sunday, we also "spring up" to hail Jesus as the Messiah. The question is whether we will get scorched when the heat is on, get carried away when the winds of change blow, or whither for lack of sufficient roots.

The heat certainly has been on the Church in recent years. You can argue, with some merit, about an anti-Catholic bias in many elements of the media and our society. But you can't argue that much of the criticism isn't deserved given the criminal behavior of a small percentage of priests and others who sexually abused children, and the complicity of some bishops and others in authority who failed to respond effectively or, worse, covered up these felonies. Will we let that heat scorch us, or will we use the light being shined on the Church to illuminate the way to better protection of children and increased transparency and accountability? Perhaps the most useful role we can play as lay Catholics is to insist that the public scrutiny being directed at the Church employ a spotlight—to see the full picture, all the good works as well as the failings—not just a flashlight directing its narrow beam into the darkest corners.

The winds of change, and even what might be termed the "breezes of trend," also have carried away plenty of Catholics. Think of how many people have decided that they are "spiritual, not religious" and have left in pursuit of the latest philosophy, practice, or belief system offering less-demanding standards or, sometimes, just better music at the services. And—perhaps an even larger number—think of how many people who you used to see in the pews around you every Sunday have disappeared not out of anger, not in pursuit of something better, but just out of a sort of fatigue. Their lives are ridiculously over-scheduled, and what with commuting to work during the week and Saturday's chores or children's game to attend, Sunday is the only morning they have to sleep in. Perhaps you'll see them at Christmas or Easter, but if you do, it's likely to be many more months before you see them again.

You have to wonder which pains Jesus more, those in the crowd on Palm Sunday who so soon turned against Him, or those today who gradually just turn away from Him. And we have to prayerfully consider how we can avoid that latter fate, and what we can do in a non-judgmental, charitable way to help relatives and friends turn back toward the Lord.

This Lent, may we extend our roots deeper into the rich ground of faith, so that when the sun gets high and the wind picks up, we will continue to shout our Hosannas, secure in the knowledge that whatever scandals may arise and whatever change may come, "Jesus Christ is the same yesterday and today and forever." (Hebrews 13:8)

For Reflection:

1. How can I make time this Lent to accompany "the lonely Lord" on the journey He is making to Calvary on my behalf? Instead of looking to Him for comfort and companionship, how can I offer Him those gifts through my prayer dialogue, time spent before the Blessed Sacrament in Eucharistic Adoration, or presence to the lonely or forsaken who are Christ in our midst?

2. Who do I know in my life who has turned away or drifted away from Christ and His Church, and how can I in a patient, welcoming, and non-judgmental way encourage them to come back to the Lord and community of believers?

3. What steps can I take to strengthen my faith so that it is not shaken in times of scandal, and so that it emboldens me to work constructively and charitably for the continuing renewal of the Church?

TUESDAY, FOURTH WEEK OF LENT
THOSE WHO DOUBTED THE FATHER'S VOICE

"Jesus answered them, 'The hour has come for the Son of Man to be
glorified. Very truly, I tell you, unless a grain of wheat falls into the earth
and dies, it remains just a single grain; but if it dies, it bears much
fruit. Those who love their life lose it, and those who hate their life in this
world will keep it for eternal life. Whoever serves me must follow me, and
where I am, there will my servant be also. Whoever serves me,
the Father will honor.'

'Now my soul is troubled. And what should I say—'Father, save me from
this hour'? No, it is for this reason that I have come to this hour. Father,
glorify your name.' Then a voice came from heaven, 'I have glorified it, and I
will glorify it again.' The crowd standing there heard it and said that it was
thunder. Others said, 'An angel has spoken to him.' Jesus answered, 'This
voice has come for your sake, not for mine. Now is the judgment of this
world; now the ruler of this world will be driven out. And I,
when I am lifted up from the earth, will draw all people to myself.'
He said this to indicate the kind of death he was to die.
The crowd answered him, 'We have heard from the law that the
Messiah remains forever. How can you say that the Son of Man must be
lifted up? Who is this Son of Man?' Jesus said to them, 'The light is with
you for a little longer. Walk while you have the light, so that the darkness
may not overtake you. If you walk in the darkness, you do not know where
you are going. While you have the light, believe in the light, so that you may
become children of light.'"
John 12:23-36

Many a homily about our recognition of God's intervention in our lives has opened with an anecdote that goes something like this:

One Saturday morning in mid-December, a man who is a lax church-goer but an avid bargain-hunter arrives at the mall to finish his Christmas shopping, only to find that every spot in the massive parking lot is taken. He cruises slowly, vigilantly up and down the lanes for 15 minutes, but to no avail. Finally, he cries out, "God, if you will help me find a place to park, not only will I go to Mass on Christmas, I'll go every Sunday for the next year." No sooner are the words spoken than a car backs out of the very first spot in the row to his right, just 10 yards from the mall's main entrance. As the man hurriedly puts on his turn signal and pulls in to this prized parking place, he again addresses the Almighty: "Never mind, God, I've taken care of it on my own."

The story provides a light-hearted introduction to a heavy subject, one whose weight is evident in the frustration and disappointment Jesus expresses when those accompanying Him disregard not only His words but also those spoken by His Father. Today, if someone hesitates to make what is manifestly the right choice for them, we ask, "What are you waiting for, a voice from the heavens?" That is exactly what the Father provided, and many following Jesus still refused to believe.

It makes you wonder if God isn't as distant and mysterious as we think. Maybe, instead, we choose to keep God at arm's length and feign uncertainty about His ways and word.

Why would we do that? One answer can be found in the instructions Jesus gave His would-be followers immediately before and after His Father spoke from Heaven. Let's start with what the Lord said beforehand:

> "Those who love their life lose it, and those who hate their life in this world will keep it for eternal life. Whoever serves me must follow me, and where I am, there will my servant be also. Whoever serves me, the Father will honor." (John 12:25-26)

Hate your life in this world to save it in the next? That goes against every instinct of self-preservation and self-advancement. We work hard to build a life that we love, and we fight hard to preserve what we've won. It's not easy, you know. It requires tremendous effort and focus.

Yes, says Jesus, I do know that. I know that an excessive concern with material gain can require efforts that conflict with the way you are supposed to treat one another. I know that an unwavering focus on the things of this world precludes you from keeping God at the center of your vision. So as an alternative to the exhausting, ultimately futile attempt to store up treasure here on earth, I offer you the chance to be honored by the Father for all eternity. If you won't listen to my voice, listen to His.

And then, after the Father spoke, when many in the crowd continued to ask questions, the Lord said:

> Walk while you have the light, so that the darkness may not overtake you. If you walk in the darkness, you do not know where you are going. While you have the light, believe in the light, so that you may become children of light." (John 12:35-36)

We know exactly what Jesus meant by those words, but there are times it's more convenient to pretend that we don't. The cover of darkness is a much better setting for some of the things we do. The light would expose too many of our flaws and failings. Against this hesitancy and fear, Jesus—who knows all of our sins, no matter how stealthily committed, and sees all of our weaknesses, no matter how carefully camouflaged—says, "I love you, knowing full well who and what you are, and in your unworthiness I find you worth suffering, dying, and rising for."

There's really nothing distant or mysterious about it. The Lord came among us in incarnate form 2,000 years ago, and remains with us today in the Eucharist and in the Holy Spirit that dwells in and among believers. He tells us plainly what we need to do: Believe, follow, serve.

We make it harder than it has to be. We swim further and further away from shore, hoping that just a little farther out the next wave, or certainly the one after that, will take us for that perfect ride we keep imagining. We ignore the voices of other swimmers urging us back in. We even disregard the lifeguard standing in his chair and using a bullhorn to call us to safety.

When we realize that we're in too deep and can't save ourselves, we start flailing about in the darkness under the surface, not really knowing what we're doing or in which direction we should go. And when the lifeguard arrives, risking his own life to bring us to the light and air on the surface, we resist him in our panic and our reliance on our own inadequate efforts. The only thing we have to do to live is to stop fighting and allow him take us to the shore. For that to happen, however, we need to hear his voice and believe him when he tells us that he is there to save us and that he *will* save us if we'll just let him do what he came to do.

The Almighty is speaking to us this Lent through the Word of God proclaimed at Mass and in our prayer. We can question what we hear and what it means. We can make it harder than it has to be. Or, like a drowning swimmer, we can heed the voice of the one who came to save us, and surrender to His instruction as He leads us to the safety of an eternal shore.

For Reflection:

1. How can I structure my life and time this Lent so that I am better able to hear the voice of God when He speaks to me? How can I adopt a mindset of faith so that I am better able to recognize, understand, and respond to God's word?

2. Which teaching of Jesus do I find most difficult to understand or accept? What factors might be contributing to that difficulty? If I did accept the teaching, what change would it require in my life, and what would that cost me in terms of disregarding my own preferences or leaving my comfort zone?

3. When and why do I prefer the darkness to the light? What things about me would cause me the most pain or embarrassment if people knew about them? Do I truly accept that, even knowing all of my faults and failings, God loves me and wants what is best for me? How can I embrace that reality and use it to heal and strengthen me?

4. When and why do I make faith harder than it has to be? How can I cultivate a greater trust in God's promise and responsiveness to His guidance?

WEDNESDAY, FOURTH WEEK OF LENT
THE BELIEVERS WHO PREFERRED HUMAN PRAISE TO GOD'S GLORY

"Nevertheless many, even of the authorities, believed in him. But because of the Pharisees they did not confess it, for fear that they would be put out of the synagogue; for they loved human glory more than the glory that comes from God."
John 12:42-43

"For they loved human glory more than the glory that comes from God."

What a devastating insight into the motive that drives so many decisions and actions in our world. It's the sort of pithy assessment that gets into your head and lodges there, a thought that keeps coming back to haunt you. Haunting, no doubt, because we recognize the role that the desire for praise plays not only in the great issues of our day but also in our own daily lives.

The Evangelist is writing here about those who "believed in him." (John 12:42) It's one thing to make status and acclaim and prestige your top priorities when you don't accept that there's anything beyond this life, anyone greater than ourselves. But when you believe in Jesus Christ and *still* subordinate the glory of God to the praise of others, the toll that your posturing and positioning takes on your authentic self is all the greater, because now you are knowingly diminishing the inherent dignity that you possess by virtue of being a child of God. Now you are choosing, regardless of whether you acknowledge it, to worship the false idol of public opinion rather than the true God. It is, in effect, an offense against both yourself and your Lord. And it is one that I, and perhaps you, commit time and time again.

John notes that the people who came to believe in Jesus but dared not acknowledge that faith for fear of expulsion from the synagogue included "many, even of the authorities." (John 12:42) How often we see that scenario played out among elected officials today.

The most obvious example is the Catholic candidate who invokes the formula that he is "personally opposed to abortion, but won't impose my religious and moral beliefs on others." Of course, this statement begs the question (although it never seems to be asked) of *why* the candidate opposes abortion. There's only one reason to object to the procedure—because it takes the life of a human being. So if you oppose abortion, and do so for the reason that it merits opposition, you are saying, in effect, "I would never kill my own child, but I don't think it's my place to intervene to stop someone else from killing theirs." Imagine if this construct was applied by a politician opposing a measure designed to prevent child abuse: "I am personally opposed to child abuse, and would never punch or kick my toddler, but who am I to tell another mother or father that they can't beat up their 3-year-old?" There's no difference in the two positions, except that with the former, the child isn't beaten or bruised; she is destroyed.

The moral plasticity of Catholic politicians isn't limited to the issue of abortion, nor to the members of one party or the inhabitants of one end of the political spectrum. How often, in the name of being "fiscally conservative" or "tough on crime" or "pro-business," do office seekers and office holders disregard the Gospel imperatives and social teaching of the Church when it comes to caring for the poor, showing mercy to those who have done wrong, affirming the rights of workers, or protecting the environment?

We don't need to look to Washington, or our state Capitol, or the news to find examples of people who have elevated the praise of others above the glory of God, however. For most of us, we need look only at our own lives. We know what pleases God, and we know what pleases others. We also know how easy it is to rationalize opting for the praise of the latter. God seems so distant and remote while the people we want to impress are right in front us. Do what they want, and we get the instant gratification of their approval. Besides, we don't want to become religious fanatics, and does it really matter to God, anyway? Doesn't He have bigger things to worry about?

Then there's the most seductive rationalization of all, the idea that there's nothing wrong with wanting to be liked and accepted. And, of course, there's not. Just as with having your sexual desires and material needs fulfilled, winning the support and admiration of others is a healthy and life-affirming thing— so long as it occurs in the right setting and context, and doesn't become so important to you that you will subordinate your dignity and your duty to God to obtain it.

As followers of Jesus Christ, we're called to take the long view—an eternal view—and to make our near-term decisions accordingly. During Lent and throughout the year, the Church calls us to re-examine our priorities to ensure that we're focused on the enduring, not the ephemeral. For more than 500 years, the Church extended that call to its earthly Vicar in a particularly powerful way. During the papal coronation ceremony, as the new Pope processed through St. Peter's, a bishop or some other high church official would kneel before him, holding aloft a burning piece of cloth, and intone, *"Sancte Pater, sic transit gloria mundi!"*—"Holy Father, thus passes the glory of the world." To make sure the pontiff got the point, this ritual was repeated three times, so that he could see how quickly the cloth was devoured by the flames.

"*Sic transit gloria mundi.*" Just like, ""For they loved human glory more than the glory that comes from God," it's the kind of phrase that can get stuck in your head. Instead of triggering regret over past mistakes, however, it can play a preventive role, prompting us to consider how meager and ultimately unsatisfactory will be the transient gain to be had from striving to please others at the expense of serving God. It can remind us, as it did so many popes, that while the things of this world pass quickly, Jesus offers us life that will never end.

May our choices and actions this Lent be directed toward—and bring us closer to—the glory of God.

For Reflection:

1. On what occasions have I preferred human praise to doing what is right in the eyes of God? What were the circumstances, and what drove the choices I made? Was the reward what I anticipated? What might have happened had I proceeded differently?

2. Does the strength of my natural desire to be liked and admired fall within what might be termed a "normal range," or do I place excessive emphasis on my social standing? Do I ever find myself cringing or embarrassed by what I say or do to impress others? If so, what experiences and perceptions might be driving my behavior? How can I approach God through prayer, and perhaps seek the help of others, for the insights and healing that will foster healthy attitudes and relationships?

3. What can I do this Lent to further embrace the reality that my dignity and value derive from being a son or daughter of God? How can I draw upon that knowledge to interact with others confidently and in a way that doesn't entail trying to "prove" anything but instead shows due respect both to them and to me?

4. What act of charity or integrity can I choose to do this Lent solely for the glory of God and with utter disregard for the impression it will make on others?

THURSDAY, FOURTH WEEK OF LENT
SIMON PETER AT THE WASHING OF THE FEET

"Now before the festival of the Passover, Jesus knew that his hour had come to depart from this world and go to the Father. Having loved his own who were in the world, he loved them to the end. The devil had already put it into the heart of Judas son of Simon Iscariot to betray him. And during supper Jesus, knowing that the Father had given all things into his hands, and that he had come from God and was going to God, got up from the table, took off his outer robe, and tied a towel around himself. Then he poured water into a basin and began to wash the disciples' feet and to wipe them with the towel that was tied around him. He came to Simon Peter, who said to him, 'Lord, are you going to wash my feet?' Jesus answered, 'You do not know now what I am doing, but later you will understand.' Peter said to him, 'You will never wash my feet.' Jesus answered, 'Unless I wash you, you have no share with me.' Simon Peter said to him, 'Lord, not my feet only but also my hands and my head!' Jesus said to him, 'One who has bathed does not need to wash, except for the feet, but is entirely clean. And you are clean, though not all of you.' For he knew who was to betray him; for this reason he said, 'Not all of you are clean.'

After he had washed their feet, had put on his robe, and had returned to the table, he said to them, 'Do you know what I have done to you? You call me Teacher and Lord—and you are right, for that is what I am. So if I, your Lord and Teacher, have washed your feet, you also ought to wash one another's feet. For I have set you an example, that you also should do as I have done to you.'"

John 13: 1-15

    True Christian humility sometimes consists not in serving but in allowing ourselves to be served.

This Gospel passage usually is invoked to remind us that those who aspire to greatness in the eyes of God must willingly, even cheerfully, seek to be the "least" among people by serving others. The focus is on the model and explanation that Jesus provides as He lowers Himself—literally and figuratively—to wash the feet of His disciples.

But we can learn much from Peter as well as from the Lord.

We "good Catholics" are doers. We take pride and find satisfaction in serving on committees, handling tasks for the parish, organizing clothes drives, donating to worthy causes, and working in soup kitchens. These are all wonderful things that redound to our credit.

But how do we respond when somebody wants to do something for us? Is our reluctance to accept born of a genuine desire "to not be an imposition," or is there a degree of ego or false pride involved when we decline an offer of assistance? As long as we're helping others, our place in the relationship is clear. If I'm in a position to help you, I'm in a position above you. My help reflects not only my magnanimity but also my superior status. Such a patronizing attitude is the antithesis of the humility that is supposed to prompt our service.

Or, like Peter, do we engage in an ostentatious proclamation of our unworthiness to be served by God. "You will never wash my feet!" That's how devoted I am to you, how much I revere you. So what's the plan here? Do we reject a gift proffered by the Almighty as a way of demonstrating our fealty, thus puffing up our spiritual pride, or do we humbly acknowledge our need for all that the Lord would do for us, and gratefully accept His graces?

Jesus had no time for Peter's posturing, telling him flatly, "Unless I wash you, you have no share with me." (John 13:8) So then Peter engaged in the kind of grandstanding that must have made the other disciples view him the way we used to look at the classmate who was so keen on being the teacher's pet. "Lord, not my feet only, but also my hands and my head." You can almost imagine the Lord fixing him with a pained stare, arching an eyebrow, and saying, "Really, Peter? Really?" Instead, as the Evangelist relates, Jesus actually said, "One who has bathed does not need to wash, except for the feet, but is entirely clean. And you are clean, though not all of you." John goes on to explain that this closing allusion to not all being clean was a reference to Judas, who Jesus knew was about to betray Him. (John 13: 10-11)

Think of the implications this exchange has for the Christian life. Unless we are washed clean by God in the waters of baptism, we will have no share with Him. That's clear enough. But in then telling Peter that the person who has bathed is clean all over and need only wash his feet, the Lord perhaps could be seen as waving us away from an excessive scrupulousness, from an unhealthy, disproportionate sense of guilt that in its own perverse way can be a sign of spiritual pride by magnifying our faults rather than our virtues. Yes, we all sin, and we should "wash our feet" through frequent recourse to the Sacrament of Reconciliation. (In keeping with the order in which events unfolded at the Last Supper, it is particularly appropriate to obtain this cleansing before we come to the table of the Lord.) But unless we're among those, like Judas, who have freely, intentionally, and with malice aforethought rejected and betrayed the Lord, we should not wallow in an exaggerated sense of unworthiness any more than we should revel in an inflated sense of our virtue.

One of the most poignant dynamics in our rapidly aging society is the phenomenon of adult children giving their elderly mothers and fathers the same care that those parents provided to them 50 or 60 years before. The parent who once dressed or bathed her daughter, or fed her son his meals and tucked him in at night, now relies on the grown child to do those things for her. Often, this point comes only after many years in which the parent has fought tenaciously to maintain his or her independence, holding out as long as possible on conceding activities ranging from cleaning the gutters to managing his own finances or living alone. Depending on the parent's temperament, mental status, and degree of infirmity, a grown child's help can be accepted grudgingly and resentfully, or with grace and genuine appreciation.

Like an elderly parent fortunate enough to have an adult child who stands ready to help as his abilities decline, we can rely on a Son who longs to do for us that which is beyond our own means. And like an elderly parent, we need to decide how we'll respond. We can deny that we need help. We can rebuff the offer of assistance. We can accept it, but in a bitter, resentful manner. Or we can have the good sense and good grace to recognize the reality of the situation and our good fortune, and accept God's gift with gratitude and humility.

That would be easy enough if the Almighty helped us directly. But God uses people to fulfill His aims, and that's where it can get tricky. Can I acknowledge that I need someone else— a person just like me, but equipped with a gift or skill I don't possess—to do something I need done but can't accomplish myself? Can I forego the gratification that I get from doing for others and instead allow another person to feel the value and dignity that comes from doing something for me?

Sometimes, we serve best when we allow ourselves to be served.

For Reflection:

1. Does spiritual pride or egotism ever distort my relationship with God? How can I best foster an appropriate—neither insufficient nor excessive—sense of my faults and failings, and a simple, heartfelt appreciation for God's mercy, love, forgiveness, and grace?

2. What is the full range of attitudes that I bring to my service to others? Are there any that do not reflect well on me? If so, how can I work to shed those and make my service as pure a gift to God as possible?

3. How do I feel when others serve me? How can I replace false pride with true humility and genuine appreciation?

FRIDAY, FOURTH WEEK OF LENT
THOMAS

"Do not let your hearts be troubled. Believe in God, believe also in me. In my Father's house there are many dwelling places. If it were not so, would I have told you that I go to prepare a place for you? And if I go and prepare a place for you, I will come again and will take you to myself, so that where I am, there you may be also. And you know the way to the place where I am going.' Thomas said to him, 'Lord, we do not know where you are going. How can we know the way?' Jesus said to him, 'I am the way, and the truth, and the life. No one comes to the Father except through me.'"
John 14:1-6

We all know about "doubting Thomas."

When he greeted the other apostles' reports of having seen the risen Christ with the declaration that, "Unless I see the mark of the nails in his hands, and put my finger in the mark of the nails and my hand in his side, I will not believe," (John 20:25) Thomas set a standard for skepticism that made a byword of his name still used by Christians and non-Christians alike.

Before he was "doubting Thomas," however, the apostle's words in the passage above might well have earned him the sobriquet "dense Thomas." The Lord knows it is the night before He is to suffer and die, and He wants to share this last meal with his apostles. Even more so, by His word and example, He wants to give them the insights and strength that will sustain them as they go out to build His Church.

161

And how do they respond? When Jesus tries to teach them the importance of service by washing their feet, Peter turns it into an occasion to show off his devotion to Christ. Unabashed by Jesus' rebuke at his bravado over the washing of the feet, Peter goes on to boast that he will lay down his life for Jesus. Of course, he eventually will do just that, but how hard it must have been for Jesus to listen to that bragging when he knows that Peter is about to deny him not once but three times. How difficult, also, to abide the presence of Judas in their company, or to listen to all the apostles' speculation when He notes that His betrayer is among them.

Despite all of that, the Lord who is about to suffer and die focuses on comforting His followers. He tells them, "Do not let your hearts be troubled. Believe in God, believe also in me." (John 14:1) He promises to prepare a place for them in His Father's house, and to take them there, assuring them that they know the way. To which Thomas replies, "Lord, we do not know where you are going. How can we know the way?" (John 14:2-5)

We often grumble that God isn't listening. He must have the same complaint about us.

Like Thomas, we're told again and again the way we are to live, the way to find happiness, the way to secure what we need. From the words of Scripture, the teachings of the Church, and the stirrings of the Spirit, we're pointed in the right direction. And, like Thomas, we listen to all of that and still manage to plead in bewilderment, "How can we know the way?" And when the Lord doesn't give us an answer to our liking, or responds in a way that we can't understand, we go from "dense Thomas" to "doubting Thomas."

Imagine being lost on the road and stopping to ask a gas station owner for directions. As soon as he begins to respond, we cut him off, bombarding him with repeated questions, asking how to get to all sorts of additional places, and insisting that he get us there by the fastest and easiest routes possible. We talk over him to the point that we can't hear a word he has to say, even though he patiently tries to help us. Finally, we drive away, frustrated at his lack of helpfulness, and doubting that he knows what he's talking about. We would never engage in such rude and self-defeating behavior with another person, yet we may be doing something not unlike this in our dialogue with God.

Lent is a season for recognizing and working on our shortcomings, and so we should identify and repent of those times when we've been dense or doubtful in our dealings with the Lord. At the same time, Christian humility is meant to contribute to our overall well-being, and to re-affirm our dignity as children of God, not to be an exercise in self-degradation. And that's why it is important to remember that both before and after he was "doubting Thomas," the apostle might well have been termed "devoted Thomas."

When Mary and Martha bid Jesus to come to Bethany to raise their brother Lazarus from the dead, the disciples tried desperately to talk Jesus out of returning to Judea, saying, "Rabbi, the Jews were just now trying to stone you, and are you going there again?" (John 11:8) When it became clear that Jesus would not be dissuaded, however, it was Thomas who pledged to accompany Jesus to the end, and urged the others to do the same, saying, "Let us also go, that we may die with him." (John 11:16) Similarly, when the risen Lord appeared again to the apostles and bid Thomas to probe the wounds on His hands and in His side so that Thomas would believe, the doubter responded with that most profound profession of faith, "My Lord and my God!"

So how could someone with enough faith to accompany Jesus into a life-threatening situation not understand His words a few days later? How could someone who had no faith in the Risen Christ immediately discard his skepticism and profess without reservation that Jesus was Lord?

We don't need to look further than ourselves to answer those questions. In the course of a lifetime—or just a week—we can go from utter devotion to nagging doubt, from understanding God's word to having it mystify us. And that is why, whether we are doubtful or devoted, we should never be discouraged. God is there for us, whether we recognize it or not, whether we meet our own standards for faith or not, and He can and will use everything in our lives to work for our own good. Consider how Jesus took Thomas' lack of understanding and plea to know the way, and gave him—and us—the path to eternal salvation: "I am the way, and the truth, and the life. No one comes to the Father except through me." (John 14:6)

For Reflection:

1. How can I arrange my life, my priorities, and my time so that I can be still and not only listen to what God has to say, but truly hear it and reflect on it sufficiently to understand God's words and will for me?

2. When have I doubted God, and how can I, like Thomas, use contemplation of the wounds of Christ to move from doubt to the conviction that Jesus is, indeed, my Lord and my God?

3. When have I shown devotion to Christ, even—like Thomas—when it involved risk for me? What can I learn from those times, so that I can maintain my devotion?

4. How can I avoid discouragement when I do have doubts or a lack of understanding, and how can I help myself remember that God will use my uncertainty to reach me in a new way, to provide me with new insights, if only I stay open to Him?

SATURDAY, FOURTH WEEK OF LENT
PETER

"After Jesus had spoken these words, he went out with his disciples across the Kidron valley to a place where there was a garden, which he and his disciples entered. Now Judas, who betrayed him, also knew the place, because Jesus often met there with his disciples. So Judas brought a detachment of soldiers together with police from the chief priests and the Pharisees, and they came there with lanterns and torches and weapons. Then Jesus, knowing all that was to happen to him, came forward and asked them, 'Whom are you looking for?' They answered, 'Jesus of Nazareth.' Jesus replied, 'I am he.' Judas, who betrayed him, was standing with them. When Jesus said to them, 'I am he,' they stepped back and fell to the ground. Again he asked them, 'Whom are you looking for?' And they said, 'Jesus of Nazareth.' Jesus answered, 'I told you that I am he. So if you are looking for me, let these men go.' This was to fulfill the word that he had spoken, 'I did not lose a single one of those whom you gave me.' Then Simon Peter, who had a sword, drew it, struck the high priest's slave, and cut off his right ear. The slave's name was Malchus. Jesus said to Peter, 'Put your sword back into its sheath. Am I not to drink the cup that the Father has given me?'"
John 18:1-11

It was all falling apart.

Just hours before, at the Passover seder, the Teacher had said that the time had come for him to be glorified. That made sense considering the adoration with which the crowds had greeted him on his entry to Jerusalem a few days before. It

167

made sense based on everything Peter had seen and heard since that day years ago when his brother Andrew had hurried to him and said, "We have found the Messiah." (John 1:41).

Peter had been with Jesus on the mountaintop when the Teacher was transfigured, and when Moses and Elijah had appeared to talk with him (Matthew 17:1-9). He had heard the voice from the cloud, with its affirmation and command: "This is my Son, the Beloved, with him I am well pleased; listen to him" (Matthew17:5). He had seen Jesus cure countless people and even raise Lazarus from the dead. And when Peter had said, in response to the Teacher's question, ""You are the Messiah, the Son of the living God," Jesus not only had confirmed that He was, indeed, the Messiah, but had assured Peter that this knowledge had been revealed to him directly by God. What's more, Jesus had promised that Peter would be the rock upon which the Church would be built, and that the forces of evil would not prevail against it (Matthew 16:15-18).

But now, instead of Jesus being glorified, and revealing Himself to the world as the Messiah and restoring Israel, He was being arrested. The traitor Judas had led soldiers and the chief priest's guards to Him, and the Teacher was being dragged off to face a trial and, likely, execution.

Peter's world, everything he had believed in and worked for, all his hopes and dreams, were crumbling, as was the resolve which had prompted his boastful promise earlier that night that he would lay down his life for Jesus.

Peter was frightened, confused, and angry. And so he lashed out. He grabbed the weapon closest at hand, and he struck blindly, not with any plan in mind, but with a furious intent to make someone else feel at least some of the pain he was feeling.

How often do we do the same when our carefully laid plans fall apart, when our expectations aren't met, or when it becomes clear that our dreams are not to be? How do we respond when a relationship sours—or fails to develop; when a job isn't secured—or is lost; when illness brings not only pain and difficulty but also robs us of the illusion that the years ahead will be carefree and that our lives will unfold exactly as we envisioned?

In those circumstances, it's very tempting to lash out, to make somebody—anybody—feel the wrath arising from our own pain and fear and uncertainty. For us, the weapon closest at hand often is the spoken word. Maybe it's an accusation that someone close to us caused our problems, or doesn't care enough about them. Maybe it's the sarcastic comment, bitter reproach, nasty recrimination, or envious barb. In other cases, we use the absence of words to inflict pain: The silent treatment, the cold shoulder, the passive-aggressive martyr act.

Whatever the specific approach, such behavior usually proves as senseless, futile, and destructive as Peter's flailing about with his sword.

Peter was scared and angry because he didn't know what was going to happen next. Jesus, by contrast, knew *exactly* what the next day held for Him. That knowledge gave Him much greater reason than Peter to feel scared and angry, and if He had decided to escape his fate, He could have summoned far more powerful resources than Peter's sword to free Him from his captors. Instead, He submitted himself to the will of the Father to secure our salvation.

Such willing acceptance of suffering is incredibly difficult, requiring Christ-like obedience and faith. No one wants to suffer, and we understandably do what we can to avoid pain. But when it is inevitable—as some pain is for all of us—why should we accept it willingly? Well, first, and to state the obvious, when the suffering we're experiencing is unavoidable, whether we accept it or not, it is with us. But secondly, and more profoundly, even when we're deprived of choice in terms of what is happening to us, we retain the ability to choose how we respond to it.

On Oct. 2, 2006, Charles Carl Roberts IV walked into a one-room Amish school house in Nickel Mines, PA, and shot ten girls, killing five of them, before committing suicide. The girls' parents had no control over what happened to their daughters that day. But they did have a choice about how they would respond, and they chose to forgive. Within hours of the shootings, members of the Amish community visited Roberts' family, comforting his widow and parents and extending their forgiveness. Several Amish families even attended Roberts' funeral. Such generosity of spirit and rejection of bitterness in the wake of a vicious massacre may be hard for us to comprehend, but it is entirely in keeping with the Lord who looked down from the cross on the men who had driven nails through his hands and feet and, rather than cursing them, asked his Father to forgive them (Luke 23:34).

There is no question that, like Peter, we will encounter pain, and fear, and disappointment, that there will be times when it feels as though it's all falling apart. There is, however, a question as to how we will respond. Like the Amish families of Nickel Mines, let us resist the urge to strike out, to respond to our pain by seeking to inflict pain on others. Rather, let us pray this Lent for the Christ-like faith to accept what the Father allows to come our way, trusting, in the words of Paul, "that all things work together for good for those who love God" (Romans 8:28).

For Reflection:

1. How have I responded at times when I have felt scared, threatened, or uncertain of the future? Have my thoughts and reactions reflected faith in God's Providence and protection? Did the actions I chose prove to be productive or counter-productive, and what can I learn from them and apply the next time I face serious difficulties?

2. Who have I lashed out at in response to my fears and anxieties? Why have I chosen those particular people, and what, if anything, do I need to do to make matters right with them?

3. How can I strengthen my faith in good times so that it will serve me well, and make me more accepting of God's will, in bad times?

Monday, Fifth Week of Lent
Malchus

"Then Simon Peter, who had a sword, drew it, struck the high priest's slave, and cut off his right ear. The slave's name was Malchus. Jesus said to Peter, 'Put your sword back into its sheath. Am I not to drink the cup that the Father has given me?'"
John 18:10-11

Collateral damage.

It's a phrase that sounds as if it belongs in a bank's annual report, or perhaps in a homeowner's insurance policy.

It actually is of military provenance, however, and its purposeful blandness disguises one of the most horrible aspects of the horror of war. The Department of Defense Dictionary of Military and Associated Terms defines collateral damage as, "Unintentional or incidental injury or damage to persons or objects that would not be lawful military targets in the circumstances ruling at the time."[*] In other words, innocent civilians killed or maimed, their families and homes destroyed, because they were caught up in the clash of powerful forces, because they were in the wrong place at the wrong time.

Malchus was in the wrong place at the wrong time, through no choice or fault of his own, and he suffered collateral damage as a result. As a slave, Malchus did as he was bid and went where he was told. On the night before the Lord's

---

[*] http://www.dtic.mil/doctrine/dod_dictionary

crucifixion, that hapless status found him accompanying the soldiers and others dispatched by the chief priests and Pharisees to arrest Jesus in the Garden of Gesthemane. He probably realized that he was caught up in a clash between the religious and political authorities of his place and time and a man whose teachings were seen as a threat to their power. He couldn't have realized that he also was witness to a cosmic struggle in which the Son of God was about to defeat, through His own willing sacrifice, the power of sin and death that would make slaves of all people.

Whatever Malchus knew, or thought he knew, about what was going to occur that night, it is unlikely that he anticipated what would happen to him. A confrontation in the dark, angry words, a burst of violence, and suddenly a person on the periphery of it all is gravely wounded. From centuries before the time of Christ to our own day, it's the people on the margins, without influence and without a voice, who tend to suffer the most when powerful interests clash. The war refugees we see on the nightly news, fleeing down clogged roads with all their earthly possessions on their backs, fundamentally are no different than the families who fled the armies of Xerxes, Alexander, or Caesar centuries ago, or those of Hitler, Stalin, or Hirohito decades ago.

But we don't have to watch news coverage of wars on distant continents to see today's victims of collateral damage. How many hundreds of thousands of American workers are unemployed or underemployed because their companies chose to bolster profits by slashing payrolls or transferring good-paying jobs here to people who will work for far, far less overseas? The owners and managers who made those decisions don't hate their former employees. They didn't take those steps with the primary aim of exposing those workers to financial and

174

emotional strain, of impoverishing their families. Rather, they had a goal in sight—higher profits—and if people get hurt in pursuit of that goal, it's unfortunate but not sufficient reason to alter course.

On an even more personal level, a woman faced with an unwanted pregnancy doesn't opt for abortion out of malice toward the child she is carrying. Rather, she assesses what is in her interests, and exercises her power accordingly. The most-powerless person in American society, the fetus, either lives or dies as a result. Just as military planners have coined the phrase "collateral damage" to describe the death of innocent civilians, the abortion industry and its apologists have been considerate enough to provide similarly Orwellian euphemisms to help assuage the unpleasantness that might otherwise arise from a frank description of what occurs during an abortion. Thus, taking the life of an unborn child is "terminating a pregnancy" and the fetus destroyed in the procedure is merely "the products of conception."

Lest we yield to the temptation of moving from condemning abortion, which is our duty as Christians, to making judgments about those who choose abortion, which is God's province alone, let's instead direct our assessments toward ourselves, and consider when, in the pursuit of our own interests, we have caused collateral damage. Let's consider when and how at home, at work, or in other settings, we have exercised our power to get what we wanted, not knowing—or perhaps knowing but not caring—who might have been an unintended victim of our actions.

When Simon Peter acted on his own, he opted for the sword, and committed an act of violence that made it harder for a man desperately in need of the Gospel message to hear that good news. When Peter acted in response to Jesus' command, and put away his sword, he became one of the Risen Lord's most effective emissaries, and tens of thousands heard the word of the Lord directly from him, and millions more down the ages have heard that word from the Church he led.

So when we are tempted to use force to achieve what we think is in our best interest, let us consider those we might harm in the process, and how Jesus would instead direct us to act. And when we find ourselves the victims of collateral damage, let us remember that Malchus was not the only one who suffered in the Garden that night. The Lord was there, and was suffering before and alongside him, not as a slave with no choice in the matter, but as the Son of God who willingly embraced suffering to redeem us.

Let us also remember that while John's account of this incident ends with Jesus rebuking Peter for lashing out at Malchus, the Gospel of Luke—who tradition tells us was a physician—goes a step further, and says of Jesus, "And he touched his ear and healed him." (Lk 22:51) May the healing presence of the Lord restore us, and all people, when the uncaring pursuit of power causes suffering.

For Reflection:

1. How can I be an effective advocate for those in the world today who suffer "collateral damage" at the hands of powerful forces? What person, or which one group of people, in particular, do I feel drawn to assist, and how can I be of help?

2. When has my own pursuit or exercise of power inflicted collateral damage on others? How could I have proceeded differently? What can I do now to rectify past wrongs? What can I do to avoid inflicting such injury in the future?

3. What can I learn from instances when I have suffered collateral damage from the ambitions or actions of others? Does some of that damage endure today—in terms of my perception of myself or others, and my emotions. If so, how can I best open myself to the healing power of God?

4. What can I do now, and going forward, so that I do not allow others to inflict such collateral damage on me and those I love?

TUESDAY, FIFTH WEEK OF LENT
PETER

"Simon Peter and another disciple followed Jesus. Since that disciple was known to the high priest, he went with Jesus into the courtyard of the high priest, but Peter was standing outside at the gate. So the other disciple, who was known to the high priest, went out, spoke to the woman who guarded the gate, and brought Peter in. The woman said to Peter, 'You are not also one of this man's disciples, are you?' He said, 'I am not.' Now the slaves and the police had made a charcoal fire because it was cold, and they were standing around it and warming themselves. Peter also was standing with them and warming himself.

Then the high priest questioned Jesus about his disciples and about his teaching. Jesus answered, 'I have spoken openly to the world; I have always taught in synagogues and in the temple, where all the Jews come together. I have said nothing in secret. Why do you ask me? Ask those who heard what I said to them; they know what I said.' When he had said this, one of the police standing nearby struck Jesus on the face, saying, 'Is that how you answer the high priest?' Jesus answered, 'If I have spoken wrongly, testify to the wrong. But if I have spoken rightly, why do you strike me?' Then Annas sent him bound to Caiaphas the high priest.

Now Simon Peter was standing and warming himself. They asked him, 'You are not also one of his disciples, are you?' He denied it and said, 'I am not.' One of the slaves of the high priest, a relative of the man whose ear Peter had cut off, asked, 'Did I not see you in the garden with him?' Again Peter denied it, and at that moment the cock crowed."

John 18:15-27

It was the practical thing to do.

Peter didn't want to be left out in the cold, and the price of admission—literally—to the courtyard and its warm charcoal fire was to deny that he was a disciple of Jesus. The maid who queried Peter probably didn't have any personal animus toward Jesus; she likely didn't even understand what was going on inside the high priest's chambers. But when you're the gatekeeper, your job is to keep trouble—and troublemakers—out, so she wanted to be sure that the man she was allowing inside wasn't associated with the prisoner being interrogated by Annas.

What harm was there in telling this maid that he was not a disciple of Jesus? It wasn't as though he was denying the Lord before the authorities, and his staying outside in the cold, dark night wasn't going to do Jesus or anyone else any good. In fact, getting into the courtyard might enable him to learn more about what was happening.

And so the first denial.

Once inside, it became clear that disassociating himself from the Teacher was not only practical, but quite prudent. All Peter wanted to do was melt into the crowd, so he could warm up by the fire and get some information. But the atmosphere in the courtyard was becoming tense. The people milling about began eying one another more closely in the flickering flames, looking for an unfamiliar face that perhaps should be reported to the guards. Maybe he had made a mistake coming inside. It was cold outside the gate, but it was dark there, too. Dark enough to afford a man some protection, and the chance to make a run for it, if necessary. But he was inside now, where escape would be far more difficult, so he had to be smart.

And so the second denial.

Suddenly things turned downright dangerous. The Lord had been bundled off to Caiaphas. There was no telling what would happen to Him. Before Peter could consider his next move, a slave approached—a relative of Malchus, whose ear Peter had cut off—and asked whether Peter hadn't been with Jesus in the Garden. His bravado with the sword just a few hours before threatened to cost Peter his life. Maybe his victim's relatives and fellow slaves would attack him then and there. Or perhaps they would seize him and turn him over to the high priest. Earlier that night, at the Passover meal, Peter had said that he would lay down his life for Jesus. He had meant it. But he hadn't meant that he would lay down his life like this, over some rash incident. He hadn't meant that he would lay down his life that very night.

And so the third denial.

And so the cock crowed.

More than 2,000 years later, the denial of Christ, His teachings, and His Church remains the price of admission to some rarefied circles. In the life sciences and other academic fields, many see belief in God as a sign of irrational sentimentalism that doesn't accord with the rigor needed to produce first-rate scholarship. More than a decade into the 21st Century, the subordination of Christian morality and Catholic social teaching to the imperatives of the marketplace remains in the eyes of many a prerequisite to advancement in the corporate world. More than 60 years after the United Nations General Assembly adopted the Universal Declaration of Human Rights, its guarantee of religious freedom continues to ring hollow in countries where the followers of Christ and the adherents of other faiths face persecution and sometimes death.

181

Fortunately, we have abundant contemporary examples of disciples who stand firm in the face of those who would induce or compel them to deny Christ. We have Francis Collins, MD, the physician-geneticist who led the Human Genome Project and now is director of the National Institutes of Health, shaping the nation's medical-research agenda. An atheist as a teenager and young adult, Collins found his way to faith early in his medical career, and since has insisted on the compatibility of faith and reason.* We have numerous business leaders, mid-level managers, and everyday employees who put their faith and its dictates ahead of profit or their career interests. And, still to this day, we have plenty of news accounts of Christians suffering for their faith in China, regions controlled by fundamentalist Islamists, and other places.

For all of those salutatory examples, however, I suspect we find it easier to relate to Peter and the terrible—and terribly understandable—choices he made that night. How many times have we kept silent at a party because it "wasn't the right setting" to share the perspective that our faith lends to the topic being discussed? How often have we contented ourselves that "business is business" and thus we shouldn't "inject our beliefs" into discussions of commercial practice or policy?

Our timidity is discouraging, but lest we despair, we should remember that Jesus knew in advance of Peter's denials, and all his other faults and failings, and nonetheless selected this impulsive, flawed, devoted, and ultimately courageous man to lead His Church. The cock's crow signaled more than the fulfillment of Christ's prophecy of Peter's denial. According to ancient custom, it also signified the approach of a new day.

---

*http://www.pbs.org/wgbh/questionofgod/voices/collins.html

Peter's new day dawned after the coming of the Holy Spirit at Pentecost, when he boldly proclaimed the Gospel and built up the Church. His course wasn't smooth, but he followed it faithfully to the end.

When someone's crowing over our failures or some other signal makes us conscious of the times we have denied Christ by virtue of our sins, we can choose to become discouraged and give up. Alternatively, we can recognize God's grace in the gift of our very awareness of our shortcomings, and we can accept the invitation of the Lord who came to save, not to condemn, to move forward like Peter into a new day of faithfulness.

For Reflection:

1. Do my words and actions enable people who encounter me to recognize me as a follower of Jesus without my having to tell them that I am a Catholic?

2. In what settings do I find it inconvenient, inappropriate, or unwise to be recognized as a follower of Christ? What does that say about me, and what does it say about whether those settings are places I should be?

3. How can I speak to my Christian beliefs in the workplace, in school, or in my social circles in a way that is clear and unapologetic, but that also is not obnoxious, offensive, or dismissive of other people's views?

4. When I, like Peter, deny Christ by means of the sins I commit, how can I balance a full realization of the wrong that I have done with sufficient faith in God's love and mercy to seek His forgiveness and move forward to a new day?

WEDNESDAY, FIFTH WEEK OF LENT
THE TEMPLE GUARD WHO STRUCK JESUS

"Then the high priest questioned Jesus about his disciples and about his teaching. Jesus answered, 'I have spoken openly to the world; I have always taught in synagogues and in the temple, where all the Jews come together. I have said nothing in secret. Why do you ask me? Ask those who heard what I said to them; they know what I said.' When he had said this, one of the police standing nearby struck Jesus on the face, saying, 'Is that how you answer the high priest?' Jesus answered, 'If I have spoken wrongly, testify to the wrong. But if I have spoken rightly, why do you strike me?' Then Annas sent him bound to Caiaphas the high priest."
John 18:19-24

When we are young, we're taught that we will get into trouble if we lie.

As we grow older, we learn that we often will get into even more trouble if we tell the truth.

The temple guard struck Jesus not because He was trying to deceive someone in a position of authority, but because He had the impertinence to speak truth to power. When "the truth hurts" those to whom it is spoken, they often respond by hurting the speaker.

And the more that a family or company or society depends on acceptance of lies to keep its dysfunctional ways functioning, the more fiercely it lashes out at those who threaten its carefully maintained fictions.

Think of the families that go to great lengths to not see a father's alcoholism or daughter's eating disorder. Think of the times we have sat through work meetings convened to "get a handle on the problem" where the problem is never handled because everyone knows—and nobody says—that the problem is the boss's son, or the boss's preposterous pet project, which he treats as though it were his child. Each election season, we see what happens to office seekers who try to offer us just a little bit of truth. Let one candidate promise that he will cut our taxes, increase our services, and balance the budget, while his opponent says that the only solution she sees to balancing the budget is to raise taxes modestly and trim non-essential services. We know from our own household finances which one has the more realistic plan. We also know that the voters likely will elect her opponent, because he's telling us what we want to believe instead of what we know to be true.

Consider the enmity the Church engenders by its insistence on telling the truth about human nature. When you encounter someone with a disdain for our religion, their first-line criticisms often focus on the abuse of children and the accompanying abuse of ecclesiastic power. Interestingly, their anger usually doesn't abate when, rather than trying to defend the indefensible, you acknowledge the horror and gravity of the sex-abuse scandal (this is particularly true if you also try to add some perspective in terms of the small percentage of clergy involved and the preventive and remedial steps the Church has taken). Instead, the line of attack often shifts to the true cause of their anger: the temerity of the Church in speaking out on matters of private and public morality.

We are told that we belong to an intolerant, arrogant and hypocritical religion, one that has no business judging others given the conduct of so many of its leaders and members over the centuries. These charges bring to mind the image of the internist with nicotine-stained fingers. Suppose you are a smoker going to the doctor for your annual physical. You don't need anyone to tell you about the dangers of smoking. You know it is bad for you, no matter what rationalizations you may employ. Your doctor, by virtue of his long years of medical training and practice, knows even better than you the damage that smoking does to the human body. Despite that knowledge, however, he hasn't entirely kicked the habit himself. So when you come in for your physical, is it intolerant of him to tell you that you need to stop smoking? Is it arrogant of him to draw upon his extensive medical knowledge to point out all the ways smoking can harm you? Is it hypocritical of him to urge you to adopt a behavior he hasn't fully embraced himself? Or is his attempt to get you to stop smoking—always acknowledging that the choice is yours—both his duty as your physician and an act of caring taken in the interests of your well-being?

The Church is an assembly of sinners who hope, by the grace of God, to become saints someday, and it has never portrayed itself otherwise, despite those who would attire us in the whitest of robes that they might have brighter targets for their mud. And for every medieval Pope who was far more worldly than other-worldly, for every modern bishop who failed morally when confronted with a pedophile priests in his diocese, the Church offers up dozens of prophets and martyrs who, like Jesus, spoke truth to power.

Our own lives reflect that mix of sinner and aspiring saint. There are times we've shrunk from speaking the truth for fear of the consequences, and other times we've felt the sting of those we wounded when we've mustered the courage to voice difficult but important realities. Today, though, let's consider those times when we, like the temple guard who struck Jesus, lashed out at others for saying things we would rather not hear. Did we strike back at someone because they pointed out a weakness or shortcoming that we've done our best to hide from public view and deny to ourselves? Did they "call us out" for something we did that was wrong or said that was malicious? Or did we, like the temple guard, act not because we had been attacked personally, but as a way of demonstrating our allegiance to—and currying favor with—someone we consider superior to us?

It's often easier to bear unfair criticism than an accurate critique. When we're wrongly accused, we know that once the facts of the matter are revealed, we'll be vindicated. Then we can play the part of the aggrieved victim, or the magnanimous soul who generously forgives a slander. The moral high ground is harder to attain when we're rightly accused. The only path to that destination is to humbly acknowledge our transgressions and try to change our ways.

No wonder we're so loathe to own our sins. And how fortunate we are to have one who, despite all the times we strike and wound Him with those sins, offers us understanding, forgiveness, and the truth that can set us free.

For Reflection:

1. What truth about my own life or my relationships am I afraid to speak? What price do I pay for not speaking it, and what price or gain might result from summoning the courage to speak? Considering the consequences that may be involved, should I first seek the counsel or enlist the aid of family, friends, clergy, or counseling professionals? How can I voice that reality in the setting and at the time when it is most likely to be heard fully? How can I speak in a way that is honest but also charitable and sensitive?

2. Thinking of a time when I lashed out at someone for speaking an unwelcome truth, what prompted my anger and actions? What, as best I can discern, were the other person's motives? Did I eventually come to terms with that person, apologizing for my actions if an apology was warranted? How well have I addressed the behavior that prompted the comments?

3. How can I better hear, respond to and support those who speak unwelcome truths in my life and in our society?

THURSDAY, FIFTH WEEK OF LENT
THE CROWDS CALLING FOR JESUS'
CRUCIFIXION

"Then they took Jesus from Caiaphas to Pilate's headquarters. It was early in the morning. They themselves did not enter the headquarters, so as to avoid ritual defilement and to be able to eat the Passover. So Pilate went out to them and said, 'What accusation do you bring against this man?' They answered, 'If this man were not a criminal, we would not have handed him over to you.' Pilate said to them, 'Take him yourselves and judge him according to your law.' The Jews replied, 'We are not permitted to put anyone to death.' (This was to fulfill what Jesus had said when he indicated the kind of death he was to die.) Then Pilate entered the headquarters again, summoned Jesus, and asked him, 'Are you the King of the Jews?' Jesus answered, 'Do you ask this on your own, or did others tell you about me?' Pilate replied, 'I am not a Jew, am I? Your own nation and the chief priests have handed you over to me. What have you done?' Jesus answered, 'My kingdom is not from this world. If my kingdom were from this world, my followers would be fighting to keep me from being handed over to the Jews. But as it is, my kingdom is not from here.' Pilate asked him, 'So you are a king?' Jesus answered, 'You say that I am a king. For this I was born, and for this I came into the world, to testify to the truth. Everyone who belongs to the truth listens to my voice.' Pilate asked him, 'What is truth?'

"After he had said this, he went out to the Jews again and told them, 'I find no case against him. But you have a custom that I release someone for you at the Passover. Do you want me to release for you the King of the Jews?' They shouted in reply, 'Not this man, but Barabbas!' Now Barabbas was a bandit.

"Then Pilate took Jesus and had him flogged. And the soldiers wove a crown of thorns and put it on his head, and they dressed him in a purple robe. They kept coming up to him, saying, 'Hail, King of the Jews!' and

191

striking him on the face. Pilate went out again and said to them, 'Look, I am bringing him out to you to let you know that I find no case against him.' So Jesus came out, wearing the crown of thorns and the purple robe. Pilate said to them, 'Here is the man!' When the chief priests and the police saw him, they shouted, 'Crucify him! Crucify him!' Pilate said to them, 'Take him yourselves and crucify him; I find no case against him.' The Jews answered him, 'We have a law, and according to that law he ought to die because he has claimed to be the Son of God.'

Now when Pilate heard this, he was more afraid than ever. He entered his headquarters again and asked Jesus, 'Where are you from?' But Jesus gave him no answer. Pilate therefore said to him, 'Do you refuse to speak to me? Do you not know that I have power to release you, and power to crucify you?' Jesus answered him, 'You would have no power over me unless it had been given you from above; therefore the one who handed me over to you is guilty of a greater sin.' From then on Pilate tried to release him, but the Jews cried out, 'If you release this man, you are no friend of the emperor. Everyone who claims to be a king sets himself against the emperor.'

When Pilate heard these words, he brought Jesus outside and sat on the judge's bench at a place called The Stone Pavement, or in Hebrew Gabbatha. Now it was the day of Preparation for the Passover; and it was about noon. He said to the Jews, 'Here is your King!' They cried out, 'Away with him! Away with him! Crucify him!' Pilate asked them, 'Shall I crucify your King?' The chief priests answered, 'We have no king but the emperor.' Then he handed him over to them to be crucified."
John 18:28-19:16

The sin of anti-Semitism for centuries has been rationalized in part by the characterization of the Jewish people as "Christ killers," with accounts of the Passion—such as this one by John—being invoked as justification for the persecution of innocent people.

The spuriousness of this charge is immediately apparent from both a temporal and a theological perspective, even though a few twisted minds in dark corners of the Internet may seek to perpetuate a libel long rejected by all people of reason and good will.

From a temporal perspective, God—in the second person of the Trinity—entered history in incarnate form to serve as the acceptable sacrifice for the sinfulness of *all* humanity. The Eternal, who created time and exists above and outside its frame, subjected Himself to all the limitations of our mortal lives, except sin, and so had to select a specific time and place to come and walk with us, to teach us, and—His ultimate purpose—to die for us and by His death and resurrection destroy the power of sin and death. That He would come to the Jewish people is no surprise, as they were, and remain, the Chosen People, and the Messiah long had been promised them by God's prophets. And that certain people within the society in which Jesus lived— acting as proxies for all of us—would cause Christ to be crucified was, terribly, an integral part of God's plan to offer all people a path to salvation.

Can you imagine people in contemporary times, or even a few centuries ago, hating and persecuting Italians as "Christ killers" because it was Roman soldiers who had beaten and whipped Jesus, nailed Him to the cross, mocked Him as He was dying, and pierced His side with a lance? Of course not; the very notion is as ridiculous as anti-Semitism is indefensible and repugnant.

And while many questions of theology may be complex and not amenable to easy responses, the answer to the question, "Who killed Christ?" is as simple as can be from a theological perspective. I killed Christ. And you did. And so did everybody who ever sinned, which is to say all humanity. The chief priests and the crowds may have called for His death, Pilate may have passed sentence, and the Roman soldiers may have wielded the hammers, but through our sins we provided the nails that pierced His hands and feet, the thorns that tore at His scalp, and the lashes that stripped His skin.

The Church in its wisdom has the congregation recite the lines of the crowd when the Passion is read on Palm Sunday and Good Friday. We're required to say aloud and in public what we so often, in effect, say when we sin in the silence of our thoughts or hidden actions: "Crucify him, crucify him." The people of Christ's time who clamored for His death were our proxies, so it is only right that we repeat their words each Lent to remind ourselves that we are united with them in sinfulness and in causing Christ's suffering.

Even a quick reading of John's account of the Passion reveals many ways in which the actions of the chief priests and the people are all too familiar to us, disturbingly reminiscent of our own words, actions, and attitudes.

The passage above begins the morning after Jesus has been arrested, and with the Jewish authorities and their retinue bringing the Lord to Pilate. They won't enter his headquarters, however, because it is considered unclean, and they want to avoid defilement as this would preclude them for participating in the Passover meal. So this group scrupulously upholds religious laws relating to purity while engaged in the foul act of sending an innocent man to a horrific death. How often do we focus on abiding by the letter of the law while ignoring its spirit, consoling ourselves that we're observing the specifics even as we disregard God's greater—and more difficult—commandments?

Consider, too, how the people in this passage looked for someone else to do their dirty work for them. They wanted Jesus killed, but weren't willing to do it themselves. They were more than willing, however, to obfuscate to get what they wanted. When Pilate asked what charge they brought against Jesus, their non-answer was, in effect, "Trust us." They said, "If he were not a criminal, we would not have handed him over to you." I suspect we all can think of times when we've pushed others to do distasteful or unjust things that served our purposes, and played fast and loose with the truth when the facts would not support what we wanted.

Pilate presents Jesus to the people three times in this passage. He showed them not the all-powerful Messiah who they had expected to come in glory to restore Israel, but rather a humble man, beaten and bruised, mocked and scorned. He gave them the power to save Jesus' life, offering to release either the Lord or Barabbas. After they opted for Barabbas, he again brought Jesus to them, saying simply, "Here is the man." The cries for crucifixion only grew louder. The last time Pilate brought Jesus forth, he said, "Here is your king." To which the people replied, "Away with him! Away with him! Crucify him!"

How often in our own lives do people present God to us, and how often do we reject Him because He is not appearing as the all-powerful Messiah we want, the one who will immediately answer our prayers, but rather in the guise of those humble souls who have been beaten and bruised, mocked and scorned? Like the crowds outside the Praetorium, we will encounter Jesus one day and be told, "Here is your King." At that point, it will be the Lord who decides who will be spared and who will be taken away. May our earlier encounters with Him ensure that this encounter results not in everlasting dismissal but in an eternal embrace.

For Reflection:

1. What prejudices do I have? How have I rationalized them, and how can I truly reject them and make amends for any wrongs they have prompted me to commit?

2. The leaders and crowd wanted Jesus to die, but weren't willing to kill Him themselves. How often do I encourage—or allow—others to do things that are wrong because they suit my purposes? If so, what acts committed in my name do I want to disavow, and how can I do so in an effective manner?

3. A wavering Pilate wanted to set Jesus free but ultimately yielded to the pressure of the crowd. Are there occasions when I have discouraged someone from doing what is right because it wasn't in my best interests? How can I best support people wrestling with difficult moral decisions?

4. Pilate gave the people a choice between Jesus and the revolutionary Barabbas, and they chose Barabbas. When have I had to choose between Jesus and an alternative? What choice did I make, and why? How often have I been lured away from Jesus by the promise of a supposedly "revolutionary" new approach to living or thinking?

5. We encounter the suffering Christ in the humbled, the bruised and beaten, the mocked and scorned. How can I best repent for all the times I have, in effect, said "Crucify him!" through my sinfulness by not helping those consigned to the margins of our society?

FRIDAY, FIFTH WEEK OF LENT
PILATE

"Then they took Jesus from Caiaphas to Pilate's headquarters. It was early in the morning. They themselves did not enter the headquarters, so as to avoid ritual defilement and to be able to eat the Passover. So Pilate went out to them and said, 'What accusation do you bring against this man?' They answered, 'If this man were not a criminal, we would not have handed him over to you.' Pilate said to them, 'Take him yourselves and judge him according to your law.' The Jews replied, 'We are not permitted to put anyone to death.' (This was to fulfill what Jesus had said when he indicated the kind of death he was to die.) Then Pilate entered the headquarters again, summoned Jesus, and asked him, 'Are you the King of the Jews?' Jesus answered, 'Do you ask this on your own, or did others tell you about me?' Pilate replied, 'I am not a Jew, am I? Your own nation and the chief priests have handed you over to me. What have you done?' Jesus answered, 'My kingdom is not from this world. If my kingdom were from this world, my followers would be fighting to keep me from being handed over to the Jews. But as it is, my kingdom is not from here.' Pilate asked him, 'So you are a king?' Jesus answered, 'You say that I am a king. For this I was born, and for this I came into the world, to testify to the truth. Everyone who belongs to the truth listens to my voice.' Pilate asked him, 'What is truth?'"

"After he had said this, he went out to the Jews again and told them, 'I find no case against him. But you have a custom that I release someone for you at the Passover. Do you want me to release for you the King of the Jews?' They shouted in reply, 'Not this man, but Barabbas!' Now Barabbas was a bandit."

"Then Pilate took Jesus and had him flogged. And the soldiers wove a crown of thorns and put it on his head, and they dressed him in a purple robe. They kept coming up to him, saying, 'Hail, King of the Jews!' and

197

striking him on the face. Pilate went out again and said to them, 'Look, I am bringing him out to you to let you know that I find no case against him.' So Jesus came out, wearing the crown of thorns and the purple robe. Pilate said to them, 'Here is the man!' When the chief priests and the police saw him, they shouted, 'Crucify him! Crucify him!' Pilate said to them, 'Take him yourselves and crucify him; I find no case against him.' The Jews answered him, 'We have a law, and according to that law he ought to die because he has claimed to be the Son of God.'

Now when Pilate heard this, he was more afraid than ever. He entered his headquarters again and asked Jesus, 'Where are you from?' But Jesus gave him no answer. Pilate therefore said to him, 'Do you refuse to speak to me? Do you not know that I have power to release you, and power to crucify you?' Jesus answered him, 'You would have no power over me unless it had been given you from above; therefore the one who handed me over to you is guilty of a greater sin.' From then on Pilate tried to release him, but the Jews cried out, 'If you release this man, you are no friend of the emperor. Everyone who claims to be a king sets himself against the emperor.'

When Pilate heard these words, he brought Jesus outside and sat on the judge's bench at a place called The Stone Pavement, or in Hebrew Gabbatha. Now it was the day of Preparation for the Passover; and it was about noon. He said to the Jews, 'Here is your King!' They cried out, 'Away with him! Away with him! Crucify him!' Pilate asked them, 'Shall I crucify your King?' The chief priests answered, 'We have no king but the emperor.' Then he handed him over to them to be crucified."
John 18:28—19:16

God can be exasperating.

We know this from our prayers, which can be answered in ways we don't understand or don't want or, sometimes, seemingly not answered at all.

Pilate knew this from his interrogation of Jesus, when he, too, received answers that he didn't understand or expect, or, at one point, received no answer.

The difference is that we approach God as supplicants, knowing that He has authority over us, will grant what we ask if it is for our ultimate good, and one day will judge us. By contrast, Pilate was accustomed to supplicants approaching him, because the Roman Empire had given him authority to grant or deny requests, to spare or take lives.

If we as Catholics acknowledge God's authority but still can become exasperated by His response or apparent non-response to our petitions, think how maddening, even unnerving, it must have been for Pilate when the prisoner brought before him didn't engage in craven pleading but rather spoke in a detached manner about kingdoms not of this world.

No doubt Pilate was used to prisoners proclaiming their innocence, begging for mercy, flattering and cajoling and angling any way they could to save their lives. No wonder he recognized that there was something different about Jesus. And that recognition provides the basis for Pilate's monumental moral dilemma.

When the chief priests' retinue brought Jesus to him, Pilate asked what charge they made against the prisoner. Instead of a specific accusation, he received the blithe assurance that if Jesus were not a criminal, they would not have brought him before Pilate. One did not become a Roman governor without being wise to the ways of the world, and Pilate must have recognized a contrived case when he saw one. This explains his first reaction: "Take him yourselves, and judge him according to your law." (John 18:31)

His petitioners wouldn't let Pilate off the hook, however, so he turned his attention to Jesus, asking whether He was, indeed, King of the Jews, and why the chief priests had handed Him over for judgment. The Lord answered Pilate's questions in entirely unexpected ways, responding to a question about His kingship by saying, "For this I was born, and for this I came into the world, to testify to the truth. Everyone who belongs to the truth listens to my voice." This prompted Pilate's query, the battle cry of moral relativists ever since, "What is truth?" When God in our prayer dialogue or His Church through its teaching gives us answers we don't particularly understand or like, how often do we respond with the same shoulder-shrugging, "Who's to say?" attitude in order to justify continuing along our preferred path?

Despite his nihilistic question, Pilate knew the truth of the situation, because he went before the people, explained that he found no guilt in Jesus, and offered to release Him in keeping with a Passover tradition. The people chose Barabbas instead.

At this point, confronted with an implacable crowd bent on blood and an innocent prisoner who refused to beg for his life, Pilate didn't know what to do. So he resorted to the solution favored by powerful people in every age when they can't get others to behave the way they want—violence. He had Jesus scourged, and let the soldiers place a crown of thorns on His head and mock and abuse Him. This brutality did nothing to resolve Pilate's conundrum, of course, so he again sought to release Jesus, only to be greeted with calls for His crucifixion, instead, and the charge that if he freed Jesus, it would mean that the governor was no "friend of the emperor" (John 19:12).

Literally shuttling between the angry crowds and the silent Lord, Pilate stalks up to Jesus and asks, "Where are you from?" (John 19:9) For purposes of contemporary usage, the question might as well have been rendered, "Who *are* you?" When Jesus remains silent, a furious Pilate asks, "Do you refuse to speak to me? Do you not know that I have the power to release you, and power to crucify you?" (John 19:10) It's hard not to sympathize with Pilate at this point. He's trying to save Jesus' life, and he's saying, in effect, "Work with me here. Give me something to go on. It's your life I'm trying to save, and I need some answers."

God already had given him answers, of course. Pilate had a conscience, just as all of us do, and he faced a dilemma precisely because his God-given sense of right and wrong wouldn't allow him to accommodate the crowd's cries for crucifixion without experiencing the pangs felt by any person capable of recognizing horrific injustice. Jesus may not have answered his questions aloud in the way he wanted, but the Holy Spirit already had answered Pilate in the silence of his soul.

Many times we pray for answers when we already have them. What we're really praying for is *different* answers, ones that are more to our liking. When God doesn't provide such answers via a booming voice from heaven, an angelic visitation, or lightning bolts in the sky, we're able to say, "What is truth?" and in the supposed absence of a response, keep on our favored way. At some level, however, we've experienced the ineffable stirring of the Spirit in our conscience, and know what we should be doing.

At that point, we face the choice that Pilate faced. The crowd was loud and clear. Granting, or just passively allowing, its demands would win him favor and assure continued power and privilege. Jesus, on the other hand, was silent or, when He did speak, difficult to understand. Choosing Jesus meant risking everything Pilate had worked so long to earn. Still, Pilate knew what was right— and he chose not to do it. May this Lent strengthen us not only to know the right, but to have the courage and strength and grace to be true to that knowledge.

For Reflection:

1. When have I faced a moral dilemma and responded in a way that was true to my conscience and my duties as a Christian? What can I learn from that experience—about what strengthened and enabled me to respond the way I did, about the consequences of my actions, and about how I can respond similarly in the future?

2. When have I faced a moral dilemma and *not* responded in a way that was true to my conscience and my duties as a Christian? What can I learn from that experience—about what caused or encouraged me to respond the way I did, about the consequences of my actions, and about how I can respond differently in the future?

3. Within my own family, group of friends, or community, what moral issue can I speak out upon—not in an arrogant or judgmental or superior way, but in a calm and respectful manner—to affirm the dignity of all people and/or the teachings of the Church?

4. How can I shift my attitudes and expectations so that when I pray, I can truly mean "Thy will be done," instead of, "My will be done"?

5. How can I best still myself to recognize the promptings of the Spirit, and strengthen myself to follow those promptings?

SATURDAY, FIFTH WEEK OF LENT
THE SOLDIERS WHO CRUCIFIED CHRIST

"Then he handed him over to them to be crucified. So they took Jesus; and carrying the cross by himself, he went out to what is called The Place of the Skull, which in Hebrew is called Golgotha. There they crucified him, and with him two others, one on either side, with Jesus between them. "
John 19:16-18

Why did the soldiers crucify Jesus?

They didn't hate Him the way that those who conspired to bring about His death did. And they didn't make a political calculation that it was in their self-interest to condemn Him, as Pilate did. Rather, they nailed Him to the cross because they were subservient to powers that dictated their actions.

Isn't the same true of us?

We certainly don't hate the Lord. We clearly know that it is not in our self-interest to put ourselves in opposition to Him. And yet, by our sins, we nailed Him to the cross every bit as much as those who wielded the hammers.

In our motives, as well as in our actions, we are comrades of those centurions. The Roman soldiers probably were indifferent to Jesus, but they had placed themselves under the power of harsh commanders who demanded unquestioning obedience and would brook no dissent. When the order came to scourge Jesus, to make Him carry His cross to Golgotha, and to crucify Him there, the soldiers weren't about to stop and weigh the justice of the sentence or debate whether they should

205

participate in this terrible act. They were going to do as they were told.

When we consider our sins—our personal contributions to the crucifixion of Christ—how often do we find that we committed them because we had made ourselves subservient to some power that had left us indifferent to Jesus? People battling addiction know what harsh commanders alcohol and drugs can be. But even those who haven't fallen under the sway of the bottle or the needle know, deep down, the unsavory powers to which they have submitted. Be it lust for sex or lust for power, the worship of money, the exhausting effort to feed an ego that can never be satiated, or the timid accommodation of an anger that resists being contained within appropriate bounds, so many of our sins can be traced to the fact that we have let something acquire power over us.

Often, it's a case of a normal, natural need or emotion that has taken on undue importance in our lives. We all need love and a measure of self-efficacy. We need the financial means to live comfortably. We need self-esteem and the ability to express anger when someone treats us or others unfairly. To the extent that those drives and emotions serve us and our well-being, they are healthy and good. But when they acquire power over us, we begin to serve them rather than Jesus. We become indifferent to Him to the point that we contribute to His crucifixion through sins committed at the behest of our new masters.

While we need to recognize how we are like the Roman soldiers in this fashion, and to work to free ourselves from subservience to forces that drive us to sin, it also is important to recognize another way that we are similar to those centurions, and to seize the opportunity it affords us to do good.

When those soldiers accompanied Jesus as He carried His cross to Golgotha they were "just doing their job."

In the course of "just doing our jobs," we find ourselves walking alongside people en route to their own occupational Golgothas. Just as Christ, the carpenter, was executed with the tools of His own trade, many people today find their work inflicting significant pain on them. Maybe it's the older worker who fears that his skills are being de-valued by rapidly evolving technology, or the woman who is the victim of office gossip. Perhaps it is someone targeted for the next wave of layoffs, or the executive who has fallen out of favor with the powers-that-be.

Those people often feel like marked men and women, and too often are treated as such by co-workers. Colleagues who were happy to reach out when a peer could help with a project or a boss perhaps provide a promotion or a raise suddenly put considerable distance between themselves and those whose jobs now are perceived as being in danger.

We have a choice when faced with such situations. Like the disciples shaken by Jesus' arrest in the Garden, we can run away and leave the hapless person to the company of those who soon will seal his or her fate. Or, in the course of "just doing our jobs," we can continue to walk with those who feel endangered and abandoned. We don't need to wage a fight to save their jobs, or issue some, "If-he-goes,-I-go" ultimatum. All we need is the courage and grace and decency to continue to engage with them, to treat them with cordiality and respect, and to abstain from all the office handicapping of when they'll go and why they're going, and how people should re-align themselves to benefit from the new power structure.

Corporate executives and their apologists like to say that the workplace is amoral. The imperatives of the market must be obeyed, tough decisions have to be made, and if people get hurt along the way, it's unfortunate, but "it's nothing personal." If we accept this statement at face value, it means that people of working age devote the single largest part of their days and lives to an activity that exists beyond the realm of morality. If we endorse this notion, it's no wonder that Christians are criticized for practicing their faith on Sunday mornings and doing as they please the rest of the week.

As individuals, it is beyond our power to right every wrong in the workplace, but a good and courageous place to start is to continue to engage with and support those who, for whatever reason, feel that their time in a job is coming to an end.

This Lent, let us walk more closely with Christ by overcoming the power of those things that can make us indifferent to Him and by walking with those who, like Him, are on a painful journey to a bitter end.

For Reflection:

1. Have I allowed myself to become subservient to a desire, force, or inclination that has made me indifferent to Jesus and led me into a pattern of habitual sin? If so, how did that occur? How can I most fully and honestly share the situation with a priest in the Sacrament of Reconciliation to obtain the forgiveness and grace needed to heal and to restore my autonomy?

2. How can I bring a moral dimension to my job, in matters large and small?

3. Who at my workplace is in a difficult stage of their vocational journey, and how can I best walk with and support them?

MONDAY OF HOLY WEEK
THE TWO CRUCIFIED WITH JESUS

"There they crucified him, and with him two others, one on either side,
with Jesus between them."
John 19:18

The cross finds each of us.

We have no choice in the matter. But when the cross does find us, we have several choices to make, and two of the most important concern our orientation—literally—toward God.

First, we have to decide whether we will turn toward God or away from Him. Many people who receive a devastating diagnosis or other crushing blow turn away, at least initially, deciding to abandon the Almighty because they think their hardship is a sign that He has abandoned them.

We have no business judging people who make that assumption at a terrible time in their lives, particularly because until we have experienced the same, we have no idea how we will respond. However, the news that we are approaching the same fate that has befallen every person who came before us, or that we must struggle with the same personal or occupational or financial woes that are affecting tens of millions of others, seems cause for sorrow, but not particularly for anger at God.

If we decide to turn toward the Lord, however, the second crucial choice awaits us.

John, whose Gospel so often includes those telling details that give dimension to the people and events in the life of Jesus, is uncharacteristically spare in describing the men crucified with the Lord, referring only to "two others." Mark likewise provides scant detail, limiting himself to terming the men "bandits." (Mark 15:27) The other two Gospels provide additional—if contradictory—information. Matthew, like Mark, identifies the men as "bandits," and reports that both of them joined the chief priests, scribes, elders, and passersby in heaping abuse on the crucified Lord. (Matthew 27:38, 44) Luke's Gospel, however, gives the account beloved by so many people down through the ages and that provides the foundation of the Christian tradition of St. Dismas, the good thief.

As Luke tells it:

One of the criminals who were hanged there kept deriding him and saying, "Are you not the Messiah? Save yourself and us!" But the other rebuked him, saying, "Do you not fear God, since you are under the same sentence of condemnation? And we indeed have been condemned justly, for we are getting what we deserve for our deeds, but this man has done nothing wrong." Then he said, "Jesus, remember me when you come into your kingdom." He replied, "Truly I tell you, today you will be with me in Paradise." (Luke 23:39-43)

The second choice is whether we will turn to God in the way that the first criminal did or in the way that the man known to us as Dismas did.

Will we reproach God for our troubles? Will we blame and challenge and castigate and even abuse Him because, at some point in the life that He gave us as a gift, we face the same trials, and eventually the same fate, encountered by everyone who ever walked the earth, including Jesus Himself?

Or will we emulate Dismas? Will we turn to God acknowledging that our troubles, while overwhelming and unwelcome, correspond to the human condition and so aren't unfair in any cosmic sense? In turning to the Lord, will we see that He is right beside us, suffering the same pain that we are, and will we also realize that He is suffering with us—and for us—not because He deserves to be or needs to be, but of His own accord for love of us?

Will we, like Dismas, acknowledge our own faults and yet have enough faith in God's love and mercy to ask Him to remember us from His place of power and judgment in His kingdom? If so, then we—like Dismas—can be assured that when our day is done, we will be with Jesus in Paradise.

And if not, if we initially turn to (or away from) God in anger, we need to remain as understanding of—and ready to forgive ourselves for—those emotions as God surely is. We need to be confident that the Father of we prodigal sons and daughters waits with joy to welcome us back, all past harsh words and feelings forgotten and forgiven.

Father Brendan Kilroy was a slight man with a large heart, one so filled with the desire to serve God and His people that it carried him from County Kilkenny to the United States as a priest of the St. Patrick's Missionary Society. This kindly man devoted the last 35 years of his life and ministry to counseling the students of Don Bosco Prep High School in Ramsey, NJ, helping juniors and seniors consider career paths and prepare their college applications. Never in robust health, Father Kilroy became quite ill just before Christmas 2011, and a few weeks later was diagnosed with an incurable degenerative neurological condition. He returned to his native Ireland on March 8, 2012 and died three weeks later in the infirmary of his society's headquarters.

Later that year, Father Jim Heuser, SDB, the president of Don Bosco Prep, was discussing faith in his homily at a school Mass. Father Jim explained that he had gone to visit Father Brendan in the hospital shortly after the latter man had been told of his fatal diagnosis, and at a time when he was gravely ill. He explained that Father Brendan told him that he asked only one thing of God—that no matter how trying his condition became, that he would never lose his faith. What a beautiful, and difficult, prayer.

Like the Good Thief, may we turn to Jesus when we encounter all the crosses of our life, large and small. And like that good and gentle Irish missionary, may we not pray to be exempted from the human condition, but rather to greet it with the unflinching faith that enables us to see that Christ suffers right beside us, and that by virtue of His suffering, we are able to spend eternity beside Him when our suffering is done.

For Reflection:

1. How did I respond the last time a cross, large or small, came my way? Did I turn toward God or away from Him, and, if I turned to Him, what were my attitudes, prayers, and requests?

2. How can I prepare and strengthen myself in good times to have the faith I need to see that Christ always is alongside me in bad times?

3. Who in my life is carrying a particularly heavy cross right now? How can I be like Simon, the Cyrenian, who helped Jesus carry His cross (Mark 15:21), and help that person along his or her own way of the cross?

TUESDAY OF HOLY WEEK
THE SOLDIERS CASTING LOTS

"When the soldiers had crucified Jesus, they took his clothes and divided them into four parts, one for each soldier. They also took his tunic; now the tunic was seamless, woven in one piece from the top. So they said to one another, 'Let us not tear it, but cast lots for it to see who will get it.' This was to fulfill what the scripture says,

> *They divided my clothes among themselves,
> and for my clothing they cast lots.'"*

John 19:23-24

"Adding insult to injury" would be an apt description of the soldiers' actions if it didn't so woefully understate the enormity of their callousness.

The centurions had just nailed an innocent man to a cross. Now, as He was suffering an agonizing death, they turned their attention to divvying up His earthly possessions. How barbaric. And yet, in this terrible scene, there is something faintly familiar, something disturbingly recognizable to us today.

Consider that we, like the soldiers, are the ones who crucified Jesus. Our sins, every bit as much as their hammers, drove the nails through His flesh and pinned Him to that rough wooden instrument of execution.

Consider, too, that we—again like the Roman soldiers—don't allow any sense of revulsion or shame at our responsibility for that gruesome act to deter us from picking and choosing what we like from among what Jesus left behind.

Each soldier took those pieces of Christ's clothing that suited his fancy. How often do we do the same, drawing comfort from those words of Christ that we find re-assuring, while ignoring His warnings and rebukes? Embracing those teachings of Christ or His Church that make sense to us, or that don't entail any inconvenience, while rejecting those that we don't understand or that would require us to change our lives in unwelcome ways?

The phrase "smorgasbord Catholic" is an uncharitable one, but as with many sayings that remain in circulation long enough to achieve cliché status, its endurance is attributable to its having some basis in fact. Originally, people who deemed themselves "conservative" or "traditional" Catholics hurled the epithet at those who called themselves "progressive" or "liberal" Catholics. In truth, however, the charge is broadly applicable. There are people who glory in novenas and the other beautiful devotions that have become a neglected part of the prayer life of the Church, but who turn a deaf ear to the magisterium's teaching on our role as stewards of God's creation. There are others who do a great job following the papal encyclicals and bishops' pronouncements on advocating for the poor, but who think that the Church is "backward" on other issues, or who don't appreciate the centrality of the Mass as the source and summit of our faith. The late Senator Roman Hruska, a Republican from Nebraska, is credited with saying that the main problem in the upper chamber of Congress was that, "There are too many Republican Senators and too many Democratic Senators, and not enough U.S. Senators." We would be wise to adapt that mindset to our religious lives and realize that the only modifier we should be using to describe ourselves as Catholics is "Roman;" all of the other distinctions and qualifiers are meaningless and work against the unity we are called to foster as members of the Body of Christ.

In many cases, our "spiritual selectivity" is more personal in nature. It doesn't involve the question of women's role in the Church, or episcopal authority, or some other hot-button issue that tempts people to assign Catholics a place along a theological-ideological spectrum as though we were engaged in partisan politics. Instead, we try to "customize" Jesus so that He meets our expectations of Him rather than our striving to meet His expectations of us. We're touched by His injunction to let the little children come to Him, re-assured by His promise that His yoke is easy and burden light, and comforted by His promise that whoever believes in Him will have eternal life. All of that is right and good, and cause for tremendous joy and hope. The problem is that if we are to realize all of the wonderful things Jesus offers us, we need to listen to *all* that He has to say to us. And some of it, quite frankly, is scary. In His parables and pronouncements, Jesus pulled no punches about the fate of those who hear His word and choose to ignore it, or those who start out on the way but don't remain steadfast in their faith.

Watch a football game on television and you are likely to see a fan waving a sign that reads "John 3:16." We all love that verse: "For God so loved the world that he gave his only Son, so that everyone who believes in him may not perish but may have eternal life." What tremendous comfort and assurance are to be found in those words, termed by some the "Gospel in miniature." But Jesus' instruction of Nicodemus didn't stop there, and we would be well-advised to give equal attention to the verses that immediately follow: "Indeed, God did not send the Son into the world to condemn the world, but in order that the world might be saved through him. [18] Those who believe in him are not condemned; but those who do not believe are condemned already, because they have not believed in the name of the only Son of God." (John 3:17-18)

As the Roman soldiers were eying Christ's possessions, they examined His tunic and saw that it was seamless. They had the good sense to realize that the garment could protect someone from the elements only if it was kept intact and whole. Tearing it into pieces would leave each recipient inadequately protected and exposed. More than 30 years ago, the late Joseph Cardinal Bernardin of Chicago invoked this image of the "seamless garment" in framing the consistent life ethic, in which he called upon Catholics to oppose all forms of killing, ranging from abortion and euthanasia to war and capital punishment.

We already are one with the Roman soldiers by virtue of our joint complicity in the crucifixion of Christ and our desire to pick and choose among what He left us. This Lent, may we emulate those centurions in the best sense by "casting our lots" for the totality of what Christ and His Church teach, so that we may be clothed with all we need for this life—and the next.

For Reflection:

1. How can I better resist the temptation to label others or myself as one type of Catholic or another? How can I best promote unity and accord within my own parish and within the larger Church?

2. Which sayings or teachings of Jesus cause me the most discomfort? What can I learn about myself from that discomfort, and what does it suggest about how I potentially should change my thinking or actions?

3. What aspects of Jesus' teachings and those of His Church are most difficult for me to understand or accept? What steps—such as talking with a priest, studying reliable sources to gain further insight, and prayer—can I take this Lent to more fully understand and embrace those teachings?

WEDNESDAY OF HOLY WEEK
THE BLESSED MOTHER

"And that is what the soldiers did. Meanwhile, standing near the cross of Jesus were his mother, and his mother's sister, Mary the wife of Clopas, and Mary Magdalene."
John 19:25

The waiting began the moment she said "Yes" to Gabriel.

Waiting to tell her betrothed that she was pregnant. Waiting to see if, knowing that he could not be the child's father, he would abandon her and expose her to scorn and shame. Waiting to reach her cousin Elizabeth, and to talk with her about their improbable pregnancies and the angel who had visited them both. Waiting to reach Bethlehem on the journey with Joseph from Nazareth. Waiting to see if they could find a room in Bethlehem, and when they could not, waiting in the manger for her labor to begin and for her child to be born.

Waiting the eight days after Jesus' birth for the presentation in the temple, and then waiting to understand the prophecy of Simeon that her son would be the fall and rise of many in Israel, while "a sword will pierce your own soul" (Luke 2:34). Waiting to see if they would reach the safety of Egypt before those who sought their baby's death found them. Waiting in exile in Egypt until it was safe to return to their native land. Waiting for three days with Joseph, in increasing desperation, to learn the whereabouts of their 12-year-old son once they realized

223

he was not in the caravan returning to Nazareth from Jerusalem after Passover.

And beyond all those events recorded in Scripture, waiting as every mother waits, for first teeth and first steps, for fevers to break and scrapes to heal, for (with pride but also sadness) her child to grow into a man.

Now, at the foot of the cross, Mary waited again, this time for her only child's suffering to be over. As she looked up at her son in His agony, the body she so long ago had folded to her breast now ravaged by whips and thorns and nails, she fully understood—and fully experienced—the prophecy of Simeon.

Waiting is both a prerequisite and an obligation of our faith, but that doesn't mean we have to like it. And we don't. When the surgeon won't have the pathology sample back for a few days, or the HR director with whom we interviewed won't be back in touch until next week, or the college to which we've applied puts us on the deferred list, the waiting can seem interminable and unbearable. And when we ask God to intervene in those matters, or even lesser ones, and we don't shortly see the hand of the Almighty providing the results we want, it's not only our patience that's tested, it's our faith, as well.

That's when it's important to remember Mary, and how often she waited for Jesus, and how her patient faith was rewarded with the history-altering role God assigned her on earth and the honor He bestowed upon her as Queen of Heaven.

In addition to being the epitome of patient faith, however, Mary also is the model of *impatient* faith, and we can learn from her example in this respect, as well. At the wedding feast at Cana, when the wine ran out, she approached her son and told Him of the problem. (Note how she did this. According to John, she simply told Jesus, "They have no wine." She didn't say, "They have no wine, and so I need you to do X and Y and Z and to follow my instructions immediately and exactly." She gave the problem to God in the person of her son, Jesus, trusting that He would handle the matter in the way that was best for all involved.) At first, the Lord rebuffed her, saying, "Woman, what concern is that to you and to me? My hour has not yet come." At that point, Mary could have given up and gone away discouraged, as so many of us do when God doesn't give us what we want right away. Instead, she maintained her faith and looked to the people around her to be the agents of God's work, instructing the waiters, "Do whatever he tells you." (John 2:3-5) And in response to that insistent faith, Jesus did what Mary asked.

Mary doesn't appear often in John's Gospel—which unlike those of Matthew and Luke does not contain a narrative of the birth of Jesus. But these two incidents in the Gospel—the wedding feast at Cana near the beginning of the account and the crucifixion near its end—yield an important pair of insights about Mary.

First, when she acted at Cana, interceding with Jesus, she did so on behalf of her host, someone who had invited her into his life and into his home, someone who had wanted her to be present at a time of great joy in the life of his family. If we want Mary to intercede with God on our behalf, we, too, need to invite her into our lives and homes. Second, when she stood at the foot of the cross, Mary didn't wait alone. A few faithful companions stayed with her to the end. When we wait at the brink of our sorrows and our joys, we can be assured that we don't wait alone. The mother of us all, who during her time on earth knew joy and sorrow beyond our imagining, is our faithful companion through all that life brings us.

From ancient times the Church has used Psalm 130, the "De Profundis," as its prayer for the faithful departed. In one common rendering, the second half of the Psalm reads:

"I trust in the Lord;

my soul trusts in His word.

My soul waits for the Lord

more than sentinels wait for the dawn.

More than sentinels wait for the dawn,

let Israel wait for the Lord.

For with the Lord is kindness,

and plenteous redemption;

And He will redeem Israel

from all their iniquities."

As we approach the end of Lent and wait like sentinels for Easter dawn and the Risen Lord, may we be conscious that Mary waits with—and for—us.

For Reflection:

1. How can I use the times when I "wait for the Lord" to strengthen my faith rather than test it? How can I turn to Mary—through spontaneous prayer, the Rosary, the Litany of Loreto, or other means—to support me as I await the joys and sorrows in my life?

2. The next time I turn to the Lord for help, how can I have sufficient faith to emulate the example of Mary at Cana, and to simply put the matter in God's hands, trusting that He will respond in the way that is best for all involved?

3. How can I more fully invite Mary into my life, my home, and my family?

HOLY THURSDAY
THE WITNESS WHO SAW CHRIST PIERCED
WITH THE LANCE

"Since it was the day of Preparation, the Jews did not want the bodies left on the cross during the sabbath, especially because that sabbath was a day of great solemnity. So they asked Pilate to have the legs of the crucified men broken and the bodies removed. Then the soldiers came and broke the legs of the first and of the other who had been crucified with him. But when they came to Jesus and saw that he was already dead, they did not break his legs. Instead, one of the soldiers pierced his side with a spear, and at once blood and water came out. (He who saw this has testified so that you also may believe. His testimony is true, and he knows that
he tells the truth.)"
John 19:31-35

The suffering was over, but not the brutality.

The witness who had stood vigil during the hours of Christ's agony on the cross now had to take in one last, wrenching scene. He had to watch as the soldiers broke the legs of the two men crucified on either side of Jesus, a step ordered to hasten their demise in case they had not already passed. Then he saw one of the soldiers take his lance and thrust it into the Lord's side. Imagine the sickening feeling as he watched metal pierce flesh, the dumbfounded amazement as he saw blood and water flow immediately from the wound.

Why does our world have to see such gratuitous violence? In October 1993, Americans reacted with horror and outrage to images of a cheering Somali mob dragging the corpse of a U.S. soldier through the streets of Mogadishu after the battle immortalized in "Black Hawk Down." Almost two decades later, we reacted with the same emotions when we learned that the Pentagon was investigating allegations that a small group of American soldiers had desecrated the bodies of Taliban insurgents killed in a firefight.

In other cases, the world is witness to brutality that, however inhumane and indefensible, is not gratuitous but serves some grim purpose. From time immemorial, the winning army in desperate, take-no-prisoner struggles has consolidated its victory by sweeping across the battlefield one last time to methodically dispatch wounded enemy combatants with spear, sword, bayonet, or rifle. And just as the Roman soldiers broke the legs of those crucified with Christ and pierced His side to hold to the timeline for Sabbath preparations, major cities prepare for conventions by having the police drive homeless people from the municipal parks and plazas where they've found a modicum of shelter. Who cares where they go once routed from their refuges? The important thing is that the city presents its best face to the world. We don't want tourists curtailing their exploration of our fair metropolis—or their spending—because they're made uncomfortable by having to walk past the homeless.

As horrible as it was, the brutality inflicted on Jesus' body by the thrust of that lance falls into the latter category of violence. It served a purpose, and not just the grim one that prompted the soldier's action.

Note that the Evangelist writes: "He who saw this has testified so that you also may believe." (John 19:35) Biblical scholars tell us that the closing section of John's Gospel includes this affirmation that the incarnate God suffered physical death for the same reason that the opening chapter of the Gospel assures us: "And the Word became flesh and lived among us." (John 1:14)

In the first decades after Christ's earthly mission, there arose a school of thought known as docetism, which held that it only *appeared* that Jesus took on bodily form, and that He was not actually with us "in the flesh." As a result, according to Gnostics and others subscribing to this theory, Christ did not suffer the physical injuries inflicted on Him before and during the crucifixion, and He wasn't truly on the cross and did not experience death in the same way that the two men on either side of Him did. Orthodox believers rejected this thinking from the outset, and it was denounced by the First Council of Nicaea in 325.

Today, the faithful are confronted with a societal belief that is the polar opposite of docetism. While the Gnostics acknowledged Christ's divinity but denied the reality of His presence among us in human form, many people today accept the historical truth that Jesus lived and taught and was crucified, but reject His resurrection and divinity. They hail Jesus as a great philosopher and moral figure but don't recognize Him as Lord and Savior. In essence, the ancient "mis-believers" accepted Easter but not Good Friday, while the modern non-believers acknowledge Good Friday but not Easter.

As Christians, we embrace the reality of both, and know that there can be no Easter without there first being Good Friday.

As Catholics, we embrace the truth of the Real Presence, both in Jesus' years on earth and hours on the cross, and in the Body and Precious Blood of Christ that we receive at Mass under the appearances of bread and wine.

Simply put, we cannot feel the full joy and freedom of the resurrection unless we first feel the horror and oppression of the crucifixion. And one cannot faithfully participate in the Holy Sacrifice of the Mass without first acknowledging the sacrifice Christ made on the cross. As Paul wrote to the church in Corinth:

> "For as often as you eat this bread and drink the cup, you proclaim the Lord's death until he comes." (1 Corinthians 11:26)

We, too, are called to "proclaim the death of the Lord" and also announce His resurrection. We are called to share what we have seen and heard with those who, in selling Christ short as being merely a moral exemplar, sell themselves short in foregoing the faith and grace that offer eternal life.

But how can we be convincing in an age when skeptics employ exquisitely sensitive tools to examine everything from life at the molecular level to the return on investment offered by an advertising campaign? If Gnostics doubted the physical death of Jesus in the years following His crucifixion, when eyewitnesses to the event were still alive, how can we expect to convince doubters today of the Real Presence of Jesus in the Eucharist?

One of the most compelling ways is to show those skeptics the Real Presence of Christ in our lives and actions. As the Paschal Triduum begins tonight with the Mass of the Lord's Supper, let us approach the table of the Lord with a renewed gratitude for the gift—on the cross and in Communion—of His Body and Blood.

For Reflection:

1. How can I offer Christian witness against the acts of violence, both gratuitous and purposeful, that I see in the world today? How can I stand in solidarity with the victims of violence and other forms of the arbitrary exercise of power?

2. How can I increase the sense of gratitude with which I approach the Eucharist? How can I deepen my faith in the Real Presence, and in the wonderful implications of that reality? How can I better prepare myself to allow the graces of Communion to be operative in me?

3. Through my words, actions, and life, how can I be a convincing witness to the death and resurrection of the Lord to those around me?

GOOD FRIDAY
JOSEPH OF ARIMATHEA

"After these things, Joseph of Arimathea, who was a disciple of Jesus, though a secret one because of his fear of the Jews, asked Pilate to let him take away the body of Jesus. Pilate gave him permission; so he came and removed his body."
John 19:38

It was an act of love so terrible in its requirements that we don't want to think about it.

We recoil from imagining the gruesome tasks of removing nails that had pierced hands and feet and wood; easing a thorn-barbed crown off a lacerated scalp; shifting a battered, bloody corpse onto a burial sheet.

As Joseph of Arimathea came to the cross that day, his mind must have been filled with many questions and doubts, but his proximity to the Lord left no room to question or doubt one devastating fact: Jesus was dead.

We, too, are called to the cross today to embrace the reality of Jesus' death and the even more-searing reality of our complicity in His murder. Like drive-by shooters brought back to the scene of the crime to see the lives taken by our actions, we're called to witness what we've done. We, unlike Joseph, know that the Lord will rise, that the grave cannot hold Him. But that doesn't change the fact that on this day He suffered and died, and did so for our sins.

"Take; this is my body" (Mark 14:22) Jesus had spoken those words just the night before, when He had instituted the Eucharist at the Last Supper. His disciples had gathered around Him then, according Him the place of honor at the middle of the table. Peter, who would brag of his faithfulness and then deny Jesus three times in the next few hours, just as we have denied Him many times. Judas, who would betray Him because of greed and resentment and other sins that each of us know well. The other disciples, whom He loved, and who would abandon Him upon His arrest, just as we whom He loves have distanced ourselves from God when the going got too tough.

Jesus is in the middle again this Good Friday, but this time in a place of dishonor where He hangs between two criminals. The disciples so eager to be at His side when the crowds marveled at His cures or wondered at His teachings, as the throngs acclaimed Him upon His entry to Jerusalem a few days before, are nowhere to be found. Only His mother and a few other women, as well as the disciple whom He loved, kept vigil at the foot of the cross, faithful to the end. His followers left Jesus and now, by His death, He has left us.

But even in leaving us, Jesus remains in the middle. Between life and death, between Heaven and Hell, between fallen man and an all-just but also all-loving Father. Those with an eye for symbolism have described the vertical aspect of the cross, its base buried in the ground while its top points straight upward, as uniting earth with heaven, our time here with eternity. The vertical aspect, they maintain, points out to right and left in an arc that encircles the entire world before returning again to meet in the middle, in the Son of Man and Son of God who hung on that instrument of death to reunite all people everywhere with God. The poetry of that description is compelling and comforting, but it doesn't diminish the brutal reality of the cross.

"Take; this is my body." I offer it to you, my friends and disciples, in this first Eucharist. Soon enough tonight, my body will be taken again, by armed men who come to arrest me in the garden. By those who conspire for my destruction. By those who will scourge and spit upon me, and berate and harass me as I stumble through the streets of Jerusalem crushed by the weight of the cross. By those who will hold me down while their comrades kneel before me not in homage with bowed heads but in disdain with raised hammers. I know what awaits, and I accept it freely, willingly for you. Let my body be broken and my life sacrificed in atonement for your sins.

"Take; this is my body." I offer it to you, my friends and disciples down all the centuries and throughout all the world. Receive it with my precious blood in the holy sacrifice of the Mass, that you might be strengthened and have my grace within you.

And we can take His body today, although the words of consecration derived from Mark's Gospel will not be spoken at the altar in any Catholic church in the world today. The hosts that will be distributed at Communion today were consecrated earlier. To drive home the reality of Christ's death and departure from us this day, Mass will not be celebrated; the miracle of transubstantiation will not occur again until the Easter Vigil.

Joseph of Arimathea approached the body of Jesus with courage and reverence. John tells us that this member of the Sanhedrin was "a disciple of Jesus, though a secret one because of his fear of the Jews." (John 19:38) The secret must have been out once he asked to take possession of the Lord's body. Joseph had to have overcome his fear if he was willing to risk his stature

237

in the community and to ask this favor of the same Roman official who had condemned Jesus to death. And his concern for reclaiming Jesus' body, for ensuring a proper burial, speaks volumes about the reverence that he brought to his act of love.

We, too, can show our love for Jesus by approaching His body with courage and reverence, not just today but each time we receive Communion. We can exercise the courage to proclaim ourselves believers even though our society so often dismisses faith as the product of naiveté or superstition. We can have the courage to approach the Lord despite our unworthiness, emboldened by our confidence in His forgiveness, love, and grace. We can exercise the reverence that proclaims our real belief in the Real Presence. We can have the reverence befitting those approaching the one who died today that we might live forever.

For Reflection:

1. Can I envision myself at the foot of the cross after Jesus' death? Would I be able to bring myself to look up at Him? Can I imagine assisting Joseph of Arimathea in his terrible, wonderful act of love?

2. Who are the "crucified" of our society, our world? How can I fully recognize and effectively proclaim the reality of what is happening to them? How can I work to prevent or ease their suffering? How can I stand in solidarity with them at the foot of their cross?

3. How can I deepen the faith and reverence with which I approach and receive the Body and Blood of Jesus Christ at Communion? How else can I show my appreciation and gratitude to the Lord for giving His life for mine?

HOLY SATURDAY
NICODEMUS

"Nicodemus, who had at first come to Jesus by night, also came, bringing a mixture of myrrh and aloes, weighing about a hundred pounds. They took the body of Jesus and wrapped it with the spices in linen cloths, according to the burial custom of the Jews. Now there was a garden in the place where he was crucified, and in the garden there was a new tomb in which no one had ever been laid. And so, because it was the Jewish day of Preparation, and the tomb was nearby, they laid Jesus there."
John 19:39-42

So much of cosmic consequence comes full circle in this short passage.

We first encountered Nicodemus at the beginning of John's Gospel, after the Baptist has proclaimed Jesus the Lamb of God, after the Lord has performed the miracle at the wedding feast in Cana and has driven the merchants and the money changers from the Temple. At that time, when Jesus' renown and reputation were in the ascendant, Nicodemus approached Him furtively, at night, for fear that his fellow Pharisees would condemn him for seeking the guidance of this upstart rabbi. (John 3:2)

We meet Nicodemus again about halfway through the Gospel, when the chief priests and Pharisees are clamoring for Jesus' arrest after the sensation caused by His teaching during the Feast of the Tabernacles. Nicodemus still is being cautious at this point, but he summons the courage to warn his colleagues against a rush to judgment: "Our law does not judge people without first giving them a hearing to find out what they are doing, does it?" (John 7:51)

Now, when Jesus has been repudiated, when He has fulfilled in horrific fashion His prophecy to Nicodemus that "so must the Son of Man be lifted up, that whoever believes in him may have eternal life," (John 3:14-15) at the moment of His apparent utter defeat, Nicodemus comes to the Lord again. This time, however, he approaches Jesus fearlessly, in the bright light of day, to tend His battered corpse.

Such is the trajectory of Nicodemus' faith over the course of the Gospel. Hopefully, such has been the arc of our own faith over the course of this Lent.

Consider also what Nicodemus brought with him: "myrrh and aloes weighing about a hundred pounds." (John 19:39) We first read of myrrh in the New Testament in Matthew's narrative of the Nativity, when he tells us that the three magi sought out the Christ Child and "offered him gifts of gold, frankincense, and myrrh." (Matthew 2:11) The balm for an infant's soft, smooth and unmarred skin now has become the embalming resin applied to the scourged, pierced and lacerated skin of the innocent child grown to innocent—and brutally murdered—man.

The Evangelist writes that the soothing substances Nicodemus brought to the body of Christ weighed roughly 100 pounds. Clearly, Nicodemus had to bear a heavy load to perform this act of love. We, too, are called to tend the Body of Christ, His Church on earth. We are called to bind its wounds and soothe and heal the lacerations caused by disputes over theology or the roles accorded the different members of the one body, or even personality clashes. This work can entail bearing a heavy load, but if we approach it as Nicodemus did—fearlessly, in the open light of day, and as an act of love—we can share with him the high privilege of ministering to the body of Christ.

Note, too, that the body of Christ is laid in a tomb in a garden.

Genesis tells us that it was in the Garden that we first became subject to death, by virtue of our first ancestors' disobedience and sin. Now Christ, the Second Adam, lies dead in a garden, but soon enough He will transform it from a place of death to a place where new life comes forth, and where the blooms and blossoms of each spring are reminders and symbols of the eternal life He has restored to fallen man.

This Holy Saturday, this fortieth and last day of Lent, is an odd and disquieting day. We are past the high drama of Holy Thursday and the horror and grief of Good Friday, but the bonfires of the Easter Vigil won't be lit for many hours.

As we await tomorrow's joyful news of the empty tomb, and all its marvelous implications, we feel a different kind of emptiness, a sense that God in the person of Jesus has been taken away from us. The Apostle's Creed tells us that during this time, "He descended into Hell." As the Catechism explains in its section on the Profession of Faith:

> "By the expression 'He descended into hell', the Apostles' Creed confesses that Jesus did really die and through his death for us conquered death and the devil 'who has the power of death' (*Heb* 2:14). In his human soul united to his divine person, the dead Christ went down to the realm of the dead. He opened heaven's gates for the just who had gone before him." (*Catechism*

243

of the Catholic Church, Part One, Section Two, Chapter Two, Article 5, 636-637)

We're in an "in-between time", which might just as truly be said of our entire time on earth. We've come from God, and we are waiting to go back to God. Today, we await the return of the One who makes our eternal return possible.

Our long period of self-denial and self-examination is almost over, but we're not quite at Easter. Since we can't speed up or slow down time, however much we might want to on occasion, let us wait patiently just a little longer in these waning hours of Lent and use this Holy Saturday as our own "preparation day."

Let us prepare, like Nicodemus, to approach our Lord confidently and lovingly, even at the very worst times, when all seems lost.

Let us prepare to care for those who are broken and bruised in body or spirit, recognizing in each of them the crucified Christ.

Let us prepare to tend the Mystical Body of Christ with devotion and humility, binding up its wounds.

Let us prepare to bring Christ into our lives, our homes, our gardens, knowing that He will re-animate them with new life.

Finally, and most importantly, let us prepare to trade our sorrows for the joy that tomorrow's dawn will bring, and to embrace and give thanks for the gift of eternal life that our Risen Lord has won for and now offers each of us.

For Reflection:

1. How have I grown this Lent, and what new insights into myself and my relationship with God has this period of prayer, self-denial, and self-examination yielded?

2. What can I do in my own community to tend the wounds of those in whose suffering I can recognize the crucified Lord? What can I do in my parish to bind the lacerations of division and discord? How can I contribute to healing in our nation, our world, and in the universal Church?

3. Having known the sorrow of the Passion and the weight of my own sin, how can I even more fully know, feel, and live in the joy of the Resurrection and the freedom of God's grace and forgiveness?

EASTER SUNDAY
THE DISCIPLES IN THE LOCKED HOUSE

"When it was evening on that day, the first day of the week, and the doors
of the house where the disciples had met were locked for fear of the Jews,
Jesus came and stood among them and said, 'Peace be with you.' After he
said this, he showed them his hands and his side. Then the disciples
rejoiced when they saw the Lord. Jesus said to them again, 'Peace be with
you. As the Father has sent me, so I send you.'"
John 20:19-21

Lent ends on Holy Saturday, and so—strictly
speaking—this slim volume of Lenten meditations should have
concluded with yesterday's essay. But Lent is not an end in
itself. It is a period in which we prepare to make a new
beginning, to lead a new life of grace, to receive the gifts
offered us by Christ's Easter victory over sin and death. So
ending this book with Holy Saturday's entry would be like a
Marathon runner stopping at the 26-mile mark rather than
continuing that final 385 yards to the victory she had longed
for each step of the way. We'll cross the finish line together on
this joyous day, and conclude not with words of farewell, but
rather with the words of greeting that Christians down through
the centuries have employed on Easter morning, "The Lord is
truly risen, alleluia!"

***

The disciples again were gathered in a room in
Jerusalem, just as they had been a few days earlier for the
Passover Seder. At that gathering, when Jesus was still with

247

them, He had said, "Peace I leave with you; my peace I give to you. I do not give to you as the world gives. Do not let your hearts be troubled, and do not let them be afraid." (John 14:27)

But the intervening days had been anything but peaceful, and the disciples were extremely troubled and afraid. Afraid enough to lock the doors.

Within hours of His assurance of peace that night, Jesus had been betrayed and seized. He had been interrogated, tortured, condemned to death, and crucified. He had died in an agonizing manner, languishing on the cross as He was mocked by His enemies and abandoned by His disciples—by the ones who now had regrouped in this locked house in their apprehension and confusion. That apprehension and confusion were only intensified by what had happened since the death of Jesus. The tomb in which His body had been placed now was empty. Simon Peter and the other disciple had confirmed that themselves. (John 20:3-10) But what they couldn't confirm, couldn't believe, was Mary of Magdala's claim that after she had found the empty tomb she had encountered Jesus. "I have seen the Lord," she told them, but how could that be possible? (John 20:18)

And so, in the disciples' moment and place of fear and doubt, apprehension and confusion, "Jesus came and stood among them." (John 20:19) Just as the Risen Lord comes to us this Easter Sunday, and will always come to us when we face fear, doubt, apprehension, and confusion. The Savior who couldn't be contained by the tomb won't allow locks to keep Him from His people. And just as the empty tomb was the first sign of His triumph over death, Jesus invites us to show the first signs of our new life by emptying ourselves of everything harmful and hurtful and destructive that we keep locked away

248

deep inside us. All the sins, and the guilt they engender. All the pain of wrongs done to us and by us. All sense of shame, inadequacy, and failure. All anger and sorrow. Let's clear that away to make room for Jesus to be in our midst this Easter season, for the Holy Spirit to find a dwelling place in us at Pentecost.

The Evangelist tells us that Jesus' first words to His disciples were "Peace be with you." (John 20:19) In the Gospel of Matthew, the Risen Lord's words of greeting are recorded as, "Do not be afraid." (Matthew 28:10) It's really the same message, because Jesus gives us peace " not . . . as the world gives" it. (John 14:27) Just as health is more than the absence of illness, peace is more than the absence of violence. The peace the world has to offer often is a nerve-wracking one that seeks to hold trouble at bay as long as possible. It's the "peace for our time" that Neville Chamberlain promised after capitulating to Hitler at Munich in 1938, and that proved instead to be "peace for only a little time" followed by six years of world war. It's the transient peace of having survived the latest round of layoffs at your employer when you know there are more to come. It's the false peace between two nations that pull back from the brink of hostilities at the last moment, but only because each is seeking a more-advantageous time to attack.

Against this counterfeit concept of peace as the avoidance of pain, suffering, and death, Jesus offers us the true peace of one who has encountered and overcome pain, suffering, and death, and who offers us not an exemption from those experiences but, in His very self, the way through them and the truth that will lead us to the life beyond them.

The short passage from John's Gospel that opened this book on Ash Wednesday focused on the Baptist: "There was a man sent from God, whose name was John." (John 1:6) The meditation and questions for reflection that first day of Lent considered whether we believed, or over the course of Lent could come to believe, that we, too, were "sent from God," and had a distinctive role to play in God's plan.

If we have any lingering doubts on that score, they should be banished by the words the Risen Lord spoke to His disciples immediately after imparting His peace: "As the Father has sent me, so I send you." (John 20:21) We, His disciples, called and chosen, *are* sent. Sent to proclaim the good news of the love and salvation of Jesus Christ to all we encounter.

Pope Saint John Paul II had been Pope for only a year when he visited the United States in November 1979 and, quoting from St. Augustine, reminded a congregation in Harlem of the identity and anthem that we who are Catholic are privileged to share with the world:

"We are an Easter people. Alleluia is our song!"

Let us sign that song with joy, confidence, and courage.

ABOUT THE AUTHOR

Mr. Thomas (Tom) Garry, OP, is a member of the Lay Fraternities of St. Dominic, Caldwell University chapter, and a parishioner of St. Catharine Roman Catholic Church in Glen Rock, NJ.

He and his wife, Sandy, have three children, Meghan, Brendan, and Erin. Tom has served in his parish as a lector, Extraordinary Minister of Holy Communion, Confirmation class teacher, basketball coach, and homeless ministry volunteer. He also has been active in pro-life and anti-poverty efforts.

A medical writer by profession, Tom also has written for a number of Catholic publications, including *Columbia*, *Our Sunday Visitor*, and the Archdiocese of Newark's newspaper, *The Catholic Advocate*. He has a bachelor's degree in international relations and a master's degree in political science from American Military University, and a master's degree in economics from the University of London.

Through Lent with John's People is an outgrowth of his (quite imperfect) practice of *lectio divina*, the ancient Catholic tradition of prayerful contemplation of Scripture cherished by St. Dominic and all who seek to follow him in the Dominican family he established more than 800 years ago.